BUILDING COMMERCE

COMMERCE BANK · STRENGTH, COMMUNITY, INNOVATION FOR 150 YEARS

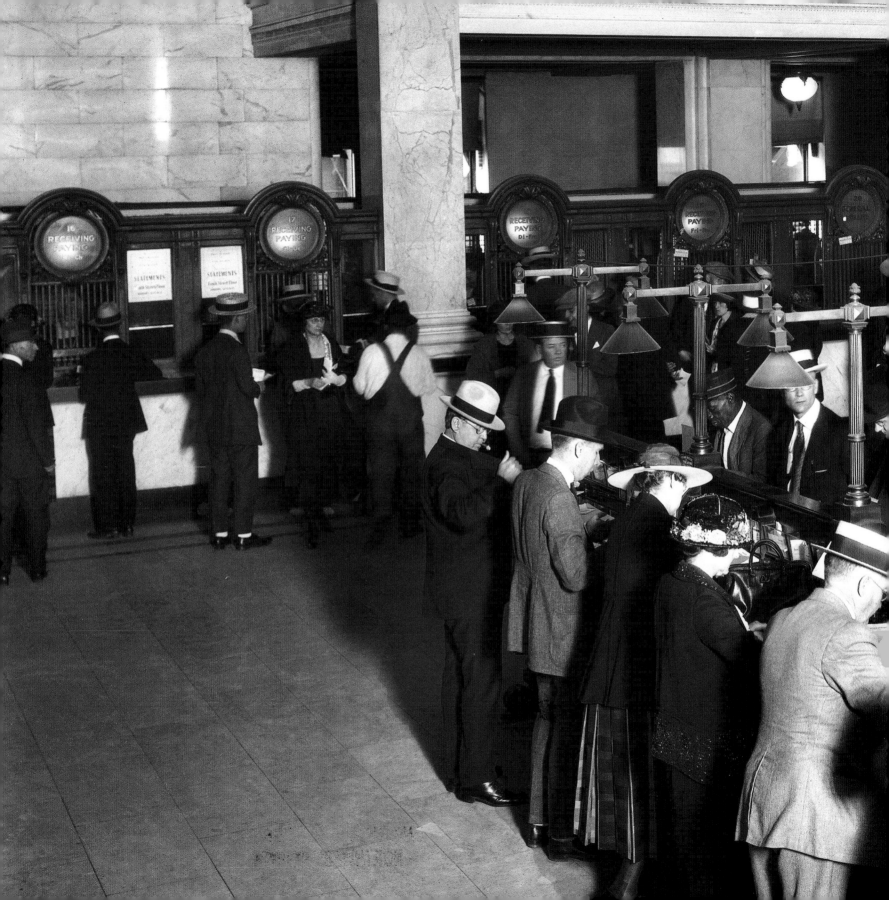

BUILDING COMMERCE

COMMERCE BANK • STRENGTH, COMMUNITY, INNOVATION FOR 150 YEARS

BY CHRIS ROUSH

ESSLX PUBLISHING GROUP, INC.

Produced and published by Essex Publishing Group, Inc.,
St. Louis, Missouri
www.essexink.com

Design by Clare Cunningham Graphic Design

Library of Congress Catalog Card Number: 2015950241

ISBN: 978-1-936713-10-3

First Printing: September 2015

Any trademarks in this book are property of their respective owners.

TABLE OF CONTENTS

SIX GENERATIONS OF FAMILY LEADERSHIP

Commerce Bank has been led by members of the Woods/Kemper family for 134 of the bank's 150 years. The following family members have held senior leadership positions of chairman, vice chairman, chief executive officer and/or president at Commerce Bancshares and its predecessor institutions.

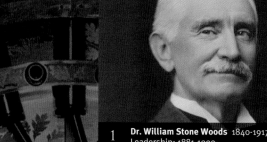

1 **Dr. William Stone Woods** 1840-1917
Leadership: 1881-1909

Gladys Grissom, Dr. Woods' granddaughter, marries James M. Kemper, Sr.

2 **William Thornton Kemper** 1865-1938
Leadership: 1906-1922, 1932-1938

3 **James Madison Kemper, Sr.** 1894-1965
Leadership: 1925-1964

4 **James Madison Kemper, Jr.** 1921-
Leadership: 1955-1991

Jonathan McBride Kemper 1953-
Leadership: 1991-present

5 **David Woods Kemper** 1950-
Leadership: 1982-present

6 **John Woods Kemper** 1978-
Leadership: 2013-present

FOREWORD: STRENGTH, COMMUNITY, INNOVATION

It is certainly the exception for an institution, especially a business, to endure and prosper for a century and a half. This book honors the contributions that so many people have made to the vitality of Commerce Bank, the communities we serve and our region over our 150-year history. We want to share our story with our customers, employees, friends and neighbors in the hope that, by knowing what has come before, we will all better understand who we are and what we stand for today.

The success of Commerce, dating back to the stewardship of my great-great-grandfather Dr. William Stone Woods, has revolved around three central themes: financial strength, commitment to community and business innovation. Commerce's financial strength has allowed the bank to reward its shareholders, weather difficult times and expand over the years, all the while maintaining the ability to operate independently. From our original base in Kansas City, we have forged partnerships and expanded throughout the central part of the United States.

A bank is and always has been a product of the community it serves, a partnership of its customers, employees and shareholders. We only succeed when our community succeeds. Commerce Bank is proud that we have continued to bring value to our customers, that we support our region's economy and that we work with others to make our communities better places to live. We have prospered by supporting and receiving support from our many constituencies.

Innovation at Commerce has been about building on our past success while looking forward. We have consistently moved into new markets and products to meet our customers' changing needs. Financial services is a dynamic and constantly changing market; we value and have been successful in applying new ideas, new technology and creativity to change while maintaining our core values of customer service and teamwork.

The book you are about to read is the product of a lot of hard work, and I'd like to recognize all those who have taken the time to help tell our story, in particular, my brother Jonathan Kemper, Molly Hyland and Terri Hurd.

As we look forward to a new generation of leadership for Commerce, I would like to close by thanking my father, James M. Kemper, Jr., for his clear-sighted and focused leadership. He led our bank for more than three decades and dedicated much of his life to Commerce. The entire Commerce community greatly appreciates his hard work, intelligence and vision in building the foundation of the Commerce of today.

David Kemper

David Woods Kemper, Chairman

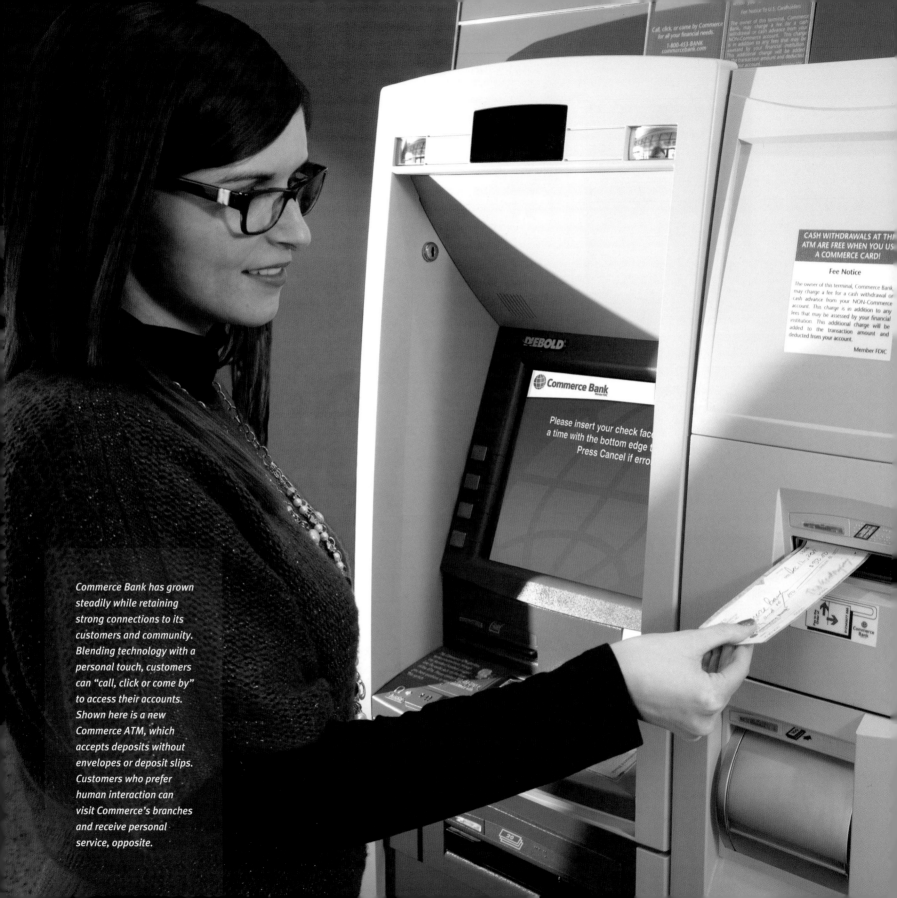

Commerce Bank has grown steadily while retaining strong connections to its customers and community. Blending technology with a personal touch, customers can "call, click or come by" to access their accounts. Shown here is a new Commerce ATM, which accepts deposits without envelopes or deposit slips. Customers who prefer human interaction can visit Commerce's branches and receive personal service, opposite.

WELCOME TO COMMERCE

The book you are about to read is the story of a bank—one of the rare entities in American business that has existed for 150 years, not to mention under the leadership of the same family nearly all of that time. Born on the Western frontier at the end of the Civil War and raised in symbiosis with the American Midwest, Commerce Bank has grown into a sophisticated bank that has been considered among the industry's best for generations.

Inevitably, the story of a bank is less a story about money than it is a story of people: of human beings who placed their faith in a dream, who saw promise in a place or a way of life they thought could be better, who had what it takes to see a dream through and of those whose means—capital, financial instruments, guidance—helped those visionaries achieve. Thus the story of Commerce Bank's success is the story of the success of its customers: the men who created one of the nation's largest lumber companies supplying timber necessary for a burgeoning American West; the visionary who built railroads from the center of the North American continent to the Gulf of Mexico and Gulf of California; the young bass fisherman who parlayed his personal passion for sport into a nationwide chain of stores; the pharmaceutical salesman who turned a calcium supplements business in his basement into a $1 billion company, purchased a Major League Baseball team and endowed the region's largest philanthropic foundation; the accountants who established the country's largest tax-preparation service; the entrepreneurs whose tireless endeavors produced the largest car-rental company in the world.

Commerce strongly emphasizes employee training to develop both personal skills and teamwork.

VALUES DRIVE SUCCESS

Over a century and a half, Commerce has succeeded by taking the long-term view and building enduring relationships to support the aspirations of such individuals and business owners—getting to know them well, helping them achieve their goals and staying with them as they grow. Those principles are built solidly into Commerce Bank's culture and into the bonds the bank has formed with its customers, be they *Fortune* 500 corporations in Kansas City and St. Louis, depositors and homeowners throughout the Midwest, a school system in Dallas, a surgical center in Colorado Springs or a family-owned agribusiness in central Illinois.

The Commerce Bank of today is the product of a single banking office founded in 1865 in Kansas City plus more than 40 mergers and acquisitions since. Over time—as the determinedly independent bank became more expansion-minded and as banking laws evolved to allow statewide, regional and then national banks—Commerce developed into a "super-community" bank with a substantial national presence: large enough to offer sophisticated products and economies of scale yet small enough to maintain a customer-focused culture grounded in personal attention, smart risk taking and teamwork.

Though the company has reinvented itself many times in response to market changes, its values have been in place and remain relatively unchanged since the early 1900s. Emerging from life on the American frontier, these values distinguish Commerce in an era of too-big-to-fail banking: strength, self-reliance, industriousness, trust, a deep sense that community matters and that lasting success is built on long-term relationships. The values and the business practices, strategies and culture that spring from them have been an important source of the bank's success and prevented many

Commerce Bank operates multiple data centers that house more than 1,400 servers and 1.6 petabytes of on-line, networked storage. Commerce uses state-of-the-art systems, processes and tools to facilitate new business capabilities and risk management.

Led by members of the Woods and Kemper families for 134 of its 150 years, Commerce Bank has been among the country's top-performing banks for the last 35 years. The bank is currently managed by,

from left, Chairman and CEO David Kemper, President and COO John Kemper and Vice Chairman Jonathan Kemper, representing the fifth and sixth generations at the bank's helm.

of the problems that caused other financial institutions to falter or fail.

Family-led for six generations, Commerce has succeeded by building on its traditional strengths in personal and commercial banking. It has been especially adept at nourishing businesses like itself—multigenerational, family-led companies—from small businesses into nationwide or global enterprises.

Commerce has been an innovative bank throughout its history, not by inventing or adopting the latest practice or technology but by understanding and anticipating its customers' needs, systematically recognizing and acting on opportunities early, and by moving adeptly in businesses that rivals overlooked or downplayed. Examples can be found in the bank's check-processing business of the 1920s; in its correspondent banking relationships several decades later; in its establishment of a private-equity investment operation in the 1950s; in its entry into the credit card business in the late 1960s and its continued innovation there, which includes the introduction of the industry's first combined credit and debit card and a current strategy that calls for leveraging strong national positions in payment systems and credit cards.

CULTURE AND COMMUNITY

Part of what has distinguished Commerce over the years is its culture—one rooted in the people-centered values of its Midwestern origins and sharpened by competition in a growing number of business sectors on an ever larger scale.

One impact of the continuity in culture is the satisfaction that employees have in their work. Independent studies show that Commerce employees are more satisfied in their jobs than people at other banks around the country. That's because, in addition to paying its employees competitive wages and offering good benefits, Commerce has a collegial atmosphere and encourages people to learn new skills, to work in a variety of positions and to continually think about how they can improve their businesses and advance their careers. Commerce also

Avoiding the Rocks

By being smart about risk, acting with long-term goals in mind and avoiding large bets on financial fads, Commerce Bank has survived every major banking crisis in the United States since the bank's founding in 1865.

During the Panic of 1893, when more than 150,000 American businesses failed, some 500 banks were among them. Commerce Bank, then a 28-year-old, Kansas City–based financial institution with the name of National Bank of Commerce, was relatively unaffected and held its position as the largest bank west of Chicago.

In the Panic of 1907, the New York Stock Exchange fell by nearly 50 percent, and rumors spread throughout Kansas City that Commerce was in trouble. While it did experience a run, the bank guaranteed all of its depositors' money. Forty-two other U.S. banks and trust companies failed in that wave.

Throughout the Great Depression of the 1930s, by far the worst stretch in history for bank failures, more than 9,000 banks in the United States went under. Bank President William T. Kemper handed out apples to customers waiting in line to withdraw money—calming their nerves and assuring them that Commerce would be there for them. The bank stayed afloat.

Commerce always strives to carefully assess potential returns against risk. "We work hard to weigh the spots where we want to invest and not invest," says Chairman and CEO David Kemper.

During the Savings and Loan (S&L) crisis of the late 1980s and early 1990s, more than 2,000 banks failed after federal controls on interest rates were lifted and S&Ls were caught with bad real estate loans. Commerce Bank, with minimal real estate losses on its books, expanded its market share.

More recently, during the recession that began in 2008, Commerce was one of the largest banks to decline bailout money under the federal Troubled Asset Relief Program (TARP), and it outperformed virtually every other bank in the country in stock performance, earnings and asset growth.

"That's one of our proudest moments," Commerce Chairman and Chief Executive Officer David Kemper said. "We got through the straits without hitting any rocks."

THE KANSAS CITY STAR.

TUESDAY, JANUARY 13, 2009

LOCAL STOCKS | Commerce Bancshares earns upgrade from analyst

Company well prepared for woes

By MARK DAVIS
The Kansas City Star

Less loan growth than expected, greater loan loss provisions and smaller profits add up to one of the best bank stocks around, according to one analyst.

Commerce Bancshares Inc. received that mild assessment and still earned an upgrade from **Barclays Capital** analyst Andrea Jao. Her "overweight" rating is the equivalent of a buy recommendation.

It's not that Jao has worries about Commerce.

Her report Monday said she liked Commerce's prudent handling of its own funding sources and capital backing. The banking company is well prepared for the industry's continuing woes.

One big plus: Commerce decided not to dip into Uncle Sam's pocket when Washington

@ Investors can get information on stocks and mutual funds free online at The Kansas City Star's Web site. Just go to the Business page at KansasCity.com.

was handing out $250 billion in bank capital.

"We think companies that have refrained from availing of government capital have the potential to grow book value more quickly and steadily than those that have," Jao's report said.

She does worry about how much it will cost banks that took government money to replace it in a few years. She also noted other pitfalls such as "directed lending."

The latter refers to the possible outcome from the growing concerns in Washington that banks aren't lending out the $250 billion in fresh capital.

Commerce Bancshares Inc.
Price per share

$38.99 $39.18
JAN. 14, 2008 — JAN. 12, 2009

Source: Bloomberg News

THE KANSAS CITY STAR

Along those lines, the **Federal Deposit Insurance Corp.** on Monday told banks it directly regulates to monitor how they're using Uncle Sam's money to support lending and avoid unnecessary foreclosures. Bank examiners will be asking, its statement said.

Commerce doesn't have that problem.

But it is a bank during tough

times, and Jao expects Commerce will continue to boost its reserves for problem loans and see its net interest margins shrink.

She notes management won't face the distractions from problem loans that some of its competitors will. But she doubts it will generate as much new lending as management does, her note said.

Earnings this year probably will fall short, by her estimate, of Commerce's likely 2008 total. Her numbers show 2008 at $2.54 a share, compared with $2.48 a share in 2009.

It includes a fourth-quarter estimate of 62 cents a share, excluding charges related to repurchases of auction rate securities that Commerce announced previously.

To reach Mark Davis, call 816-234-4372 or send e-mail to mdavis@kcstar.com.

Commerce Bank seeks to build valued, long-term relationships with customers of virtually every size and type. Using a Commerce electronic payment system to pay vendors has helped the Mesquite Independent School District in Texas, right, save money. Opposite, Alefs Harley-Davidson in Wichita, Kansas, built a 58,000-square-foot showroom with financing from Commerce.

gives managers of its business lines and local operations a significant amount of autonomy.

For more than a quarter-century, the behavior of Commerce's people has been defined by several principles. As Commerce Chairman and CEO David Kemper described them, they are: be accessible, focus on the customer, be good to each other and consider the long run. "We win on the playing field and don't look at the scoreboard," he said.

From the beginning, Commerce, its executives and employees have worked to improve the quality of life in the towns and cities where the bank operates, typically without seeking attention or recognition. The company and its charitable foundations support museums and arts organizations, libraries, botanical gardens and universities; employees volunteer their time with innumerable social and cultural non-profits. Commerce's executives believe that the bank prospers when the cities and towns in which it resides prosper.

As Commerce Bank begins its second sesquicentennial, it is planning for the future of banking and striving, as always, to find more ways to create value for its customers. After 150 years, Commerce remains a bank that understands what its communities need and consistently meets those needs with innovative products and services along with the assurance that it will be there as a partner for the long term.

Commerce Bank's leaders note that the bank's strength reflects the vitality of the communities in which it operates. Among the many beneficiaries of Commerce's community support is the Commerce Bank Center for Science Education, the focal point of education and sustainability programming at the Missouri Botanical Garden, above, in St. Louis.

In reading this book, you'll encounter many people who were responsible for the settlement and growth of the western half of the United States, the development of the modern banking system and maturation of the nation's economy, and the success of Commerce's communities along with that of the bank itself. One of them is Harry Truman, the 33rd U.S. president, who worked for Commerce as a clerk and cashier in the early 1900s. Truman described the bank's formative leader—and perhaps captured the essence of Commerce itself—when he said of the famously assiduous Dr. William Woods, "There are dozens of stories about his close accounting of the nickels and the pennies, but if he chose to back a man, he stayed with him through thick and thin if that man had energy and character."

Commerce employees came out in force to show support for the Kansas City Royals baseball team during its run to the 2014 World Series. Commerce has provided the Royals with a broad array of financial services—and has been a loyal sponsor—since the Royals joined Major League Baseball as an expansion team in 1969.

An estimated quarter million pioneers passed through the Appalachians westward into the Ohio and Mississippi River valleys in the late 1700s and early 1800s, settling what would eventually become the American Midwest. Among the earliest pioneers was Daniel Boone, shown in this oil painting by Missouri artist George Caleb Bingham escorting settlers into western Kentucky through the Cumberland Gap.

ORIGINS

Commerce Bank's earliest chapter tells of the region in which the bank was founded and still has its principal operations. It is the story of the settlement and development of the American West following American independence.

Starting in the late 1700s, a wave of European descendants spread westward to the Kentucky and the Ohio River valleys through the Cumberland Gap, flooding the western side of the Appalachian mountains with settlers. Settlement initially stopped at the eastern shores of the Mississippi River, as Louisiana and the western side of the Mississippi Valley was foreign land claimed variously by Spain or France since the time of La Salle and Marquette a century earlier.

In 1803, however, Napoleon abandoned his dreams of a French North American empire and offered the Louisiana territory to the United States. The Louisiana Purchase was heavily debated as the government wrestled with how to defend, govern and serve an already large and dispersed nation. Referring to the territory that would one day be the home of Commerce Bank, Alexander Hamilton worried that, "As to the unbounded region west of the Mississippi, it is, with the exception of a very few settlements of Spaniards and Frenchmen bordering on the banks of the river, a wilderness through which wander numerous tribes of Indians. And when we consider the present extent of the United States, and that not one-sixteenth part of its territory is yet under occupation, the advantage of the acquisition, as it relates to actual settlement, appears too distant and remote to strike the mind of a sober politician with much force."

The first settlers in this region, beginning in the 5th century, were various Native American peoples, including the Hopewell and Mississippian cultures, who lived in the Mississippi and Missouri valleys where Kansas City and St. Louis now are. They built communities still evidenced by impressive earthworks such as the Cahokia Mounds, a UNESCO world heritage site 10 miles east of St. Louis. This single settlement was the largest pre-Columbian urban population north of the Aztec cities in Mexico, with an estimated 10,000-plus inhabitants at its peak between 1050 and 1150. This map shows Indian territories at the western boundary of the United States in 1837.

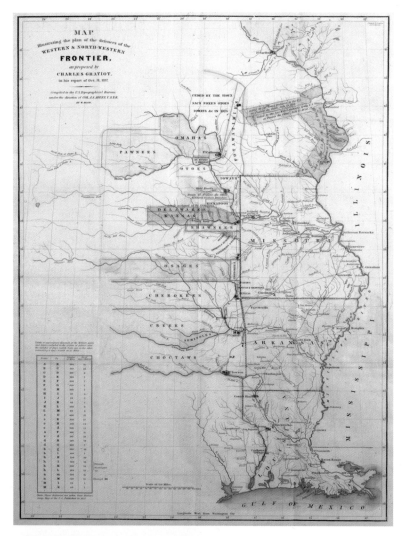

Francis Reid Long, who arrived in Kansas City from Kentucky in 1850, founded Commerce Bank's first predecessor.

BIRTH OF THE MIDWEST

With this defining acquisition, America became a continental nation: the Louisiana Purchase's 800,000 square miles doubled American land area and assured the country of control of navigation and commerce down the Mississippi River and into the Gulf of Mexico.

Jefferson dispatched his personal secretary, Meriwether Lewis, to map the new territory with his co-commander William Clark, paving the way for Americans to push deep into that hinterland. There, they found rich farmland and abundant minerals and wildlife—resources that further drew Easterners, their migrations made easier when the threat of attacks by Native Americans subsided following the War of 1812. As wave after wave of immigrants swelled its population, the region became rich in people, rich in natural resources and rich in potential—but chronically short of capital. It would later take banks to channel capital and credit into the area, facilitating the development of its infrastructure and industry.

The State of Missouri joined the union in 1821 as the country's largest state by territory, its identity shaped and defined by the two largest rivers on the North American continent—the Mississippi and the Missouri. Because of this strategic location, Missouri would play an important role in the economic development of the new Midwest as well as that of the West and, eventually, the country as a whole. In tribute to the still-living third American president and his grand vision for the potential of an American West, when Missouri's leaders decided to relocate the capital from St. Charles to the geographic center of the new state, they chose to name it Jefferson City.

By the early 1800s, many posts and towns had been established along the Mississippi and Missouri rivers, and St. Louis in particular had become the region's main trading capital. Situated below the confluence of the two great rivers, St. Louis grew into America's eighth largest city by the 1850s. It was a major economic hub whose docks were bustling with business as steamboats carried corn, wheat, tobacco and beef south to the Port of New Orleans. Crops and supplies from the north and east landed on those docks, to be distributed by merchants to the region's growing population.

Some 250 miles to the west, on rocky bluffs that Captain William Clark had described as offering "a Commanding Situation for a fort," another economic hub was emerging on the south banks of the Missouri: the town that would become Kansas City. Following the resettlements of Native American tribes from the eastern United States into what are now Kansas, Oklahoma and Nebraska, a brisk business emerged trading goods with the Indian communities. Overland trade along the Oregon, Santa Fe and California trails—and, later, railroads—carried settlers and adventurers from the Kansas City area across Indian land to the Pacific Northwest and into former Mexican territory: today's Oregon, California and New Mexico.

The discovery of gold in California in 1848 reinforced the region's position as the country's crossroads and the realization that the Great Plains themselves had the resources to support agriculture and further settlement.

With its quickly expanding population (2,500 at the time it was incorporated in 1850), Kansas City was the starting point for the West, a place of rapid growth, vigorous commerce and seemingly unbounded promise. As such, it required services to support trade and to fund new ventures such as stores, warehouses, transportation infrastructure and factories.

It was in this setting that a man from Woodford County, Kentucky, took the first steps toward the founding of what we know today as Commerce Bank. Francis Reid Long climbed out of a stagecoach and onto the dusty streets of the newly chartered Town of Kansas in 1850, determined to start a bank. If he had listened to his wife, Drusilla, however, he might never have put down roots, let alone open a bank that would evolve into one of the region's largest. Mrs. Long called her new home "the most Godforsaken place I've ever seen." Though she wasn't far

off the mark given the state of affairs at the time of her arrival, it wouldn't be long before the Town of Kansas became a city and then that city one of the nation's most important transportation and communication centers— and one that would later be distinguished for its beautiful neighborhoods and boulevards.

In 1873, Commerce moved into its second bank office, located at the corner of Fourth and Delaware streets in Kansas City. The Magnolia Saloon operated in the bank's basement.

Following the 1869 opening of the Hannibal Bridge, Kansas City established itself as an important regional distribution center. New railroads brought cattle to slaughter in Kansas City and carried them in refrigerated boxcars to the East for further processing. Grain companies, lumber dealers, grocers and dry goods wholesalers sprouted to serve the growing region; this 1867 photograph shows the southeast corner of Third and Main streets, looking east.

RIDING GROWTH TO PROSPERITY

Even in established communities, banking was not the most secure or stable profession in the mid-1800s. Many banks started as private ventures of well-known merchants and in many cases had precarious balance sheets stuffed with questionable IOUs, dubious bonds and mortgages. Missouri avoided the "wildcat" banks; its state constitution of 1821 initially contemplated a single, state-owned bank: the State Bank of Missouri, which was chartered in 1837, with a main banking office in St. Louis and branches in six other towns.

Legislation passed by the federal government in 1863 and 1864, largely to fund the Civil War effort, promoted the issuance of federal paper currency and created nationally chartered banks. Banks with national charters could issue their own notes backed by U.S. Treasury bonds (a practice that continued until 1935). In addition to the name and signature of the U.S. Comptroller of the Currency, these national bank notes carried the name of the issuing bank and the signatures of that bank's treasurer and president.

The Civil War, fought from 1861 to 1865, nearly tore the country apart over slavery and issues of governance. To this day, it remains the deadliest war in U.S. history, with an estimated 750,000 Americans losing their lives. Missouri's role in the war was a central one, and the Kansas City area was the scene of decisive events in the years leading up to the war as well as toward its conclusion.

Following the Civil War, the United States economy grew at an unprecedented rate. Against that backdrop, Francis Reid Long started his bank, and it rode the city's growth to prosperity. With $10,000 in capital, Long joined with A. S. Branham, a member of his wife's family, and Nathaniel Grant in 1865 to establish Long, Grant & Company, which became the Kansas City Savings Association. They located their first office at the corner of Second and Main streets before moving their banking house in 1873 to Fourth and Delaware, where the Magnolia Saloon occupied the basement. One of the first depositors was J. K. Davidson, later a prominent Kansas City grain trader.

Railroads were essential to the growth of the Midwest in the late 1800s, and Kansas City developed into the region's major transportation hub. Below, members of Kansas City's Commercial Club, forerunner to the Chamber of Commerce, pose on their annual train trip to Chicago to promote their city.

The city's population increased from 32,000 in 1869, when Long became mayor, to 56,000 a decade later (it would be 133,000 ten years after that). The growth was fueled in large part by the Hannibal Bridge, which opened in 1869 as the first Missouri River crossing and established Kansas City as the region's major rail and industrial center. Following the development of railroads, the Kansas City Stockyards opened in 1871, and by the 1880s, eight major meatpacking houses were located in Kansas City, employing some 6,500 workers.

Wheat contributed significantly to the growth, as Kansas City is situated in what has become one of the world's most important grain-producing regions. The nation's first "grain call" was issued in Kansas City in 1876, marking the start of the trading of grain as a commodities future. Trading was conducted on the floor of the Kansas City Board of Trade, a clearinghouse started in the 1850s by a group of local merchants.

SAFE BANKING IN AN UNCERTAIN TIME

The Kansas City Savings Association benefited from the region's growth and strong economic conditions and conducted business with a conservative philosophy: it was eager to help companies start up or expand, but it also kept close tabs on its loans. In an 1878 newspaper advertisement, the bank offered to buy commercial paper and to provide advances on bills of lading—noting that the bank "extends to its customers all the accommodations consistent with safe banking." Reported capital was $50,000, and deposits were $250,000 that year.

While the Kansas City Savings Association practiced safe lending habits, the banking environment within which it operated was still sometimes that of the wild west. There were few guarantees that any of the businesses the bank supported would survive, let alone thrive, and regulation of state-chartered banks was minimal: Missouri didn't

Early American Banking

When banking was first practiced in the United States, its development followed a different sequence than it had in Europe. Europe had wealth and capital before it had banks, and banks were created to put that idle capital to work; a financially challenged United States used banks to pool resources and bank credit as a bootstrap to *build* wealth and capital.

Author Bray Hammond stated this clearly in his writings on banking's origins: "American banking differed ... from Old World banking in that it originated in a want of capital, not in a surplus of it," he wrote in his Pulitzer Prize–winning, 1957 book *Banks and Politics in America from the Revolution to the Civil War.* "European economies were already mature when their first banks arose, and they possessed age-old accumulations of wealth upon which those banks could rest. In England, stores of coin and plate had been lodged with goldsmiths, and the goldsmiths had turned bankers to find a use for the treasure. Nothing of the sort happened in America ... Needs were great, means were few, and men were resourceful. The implusion to which they responded was that of demand, not supply, and their response was to club together their scanty funds ... and form institutions that should do for them collectively what they could not do severally."

The first bank in the United States was formed in 1781 when Congress chartered the Bank of North America, based in Philadelphia. Three years later, Boston merchants started the Massachusetts Bank, and Alexander Hamilton helped form the Bank of

New York. From the start, there was considerable distrust of banks in this country, rooted in the Jeffersonian notion that a great democratic country would emerge from the freedom and independence of self-sufficient farmers. Hamilton argued on the contrary for a stronger central government and a banking system that could support the new nation's needs to provide sound credit and a stable currency.

In Missouri, private capital banking—as distinguished from government-controlled banks— wasn't permitted until the state constitution was amended in 1857. Prior to that time, the State Bank of Missouri—owned and controlled by the state itself— held a monopoly charter from its establishment in 1837. The 1857 legislation allowed nine Missouri banks,

and by 1859, all were in operation; seven had their headquarters in St. Louis. The State Bank existed until 1866, when the state's interest was sold and all of the bank's 10 branches became nationally chartered banks.

Banking spawned its own terminology that can be both familiar and somewhat strange. For example, on banks' balance sheets, customers' "deposits" are liabilities, not assets; and "cash" and "investments" are considered non- or low-earning reserves. Perhaps most peculiar is the power of banks to "create" deposits as they "credit" their own deposit ledgers with the proceeds of their loans to customers.

All of this works if a bank holds public confidence that it can make timely payment on its obligations, including return of depositors' funds. Generally, this is accomplished by the prudence with which management operates a bank—particularly the holding of sufficient levels of capital and cash reserves to conduct daily business, accommodate occasional losses and withstand public panics and depositor runs.

Like other nationally chartered banks, Commerce issued its own currency, backed by U.S. government bonds and personally signed by the bank's president. The National Bank of Commerce notes from the early 1900s, above, were signed by Dr. William Woods and J. W. Perry.

Dr. William Stone Woods bought a controlling interest in the Kansas City Savings Association, Commerce's forerunner, in 1881. He became president, changed the name to Bank of Commerce and infused the institution with his vision of what a bank, and a banker, should do for the local community—attested to by an 1893 letter, below, to his nephew Jesse Rubey, who was starting a bank in Leadville, Colorado.

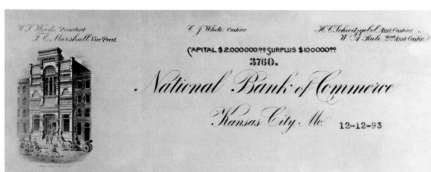

require banks to incorporate until 1877 and didn't pass laws regulating banks until 1891.

Moreover, banking was tedious, manual work. The bank's loan and deposit ledgers were kept in longhand, and statements written in pen were proofed by employees who performed calculations without the aid of machines and shouted the numbers out to each other. Sometimes bank work was literally "heavy lifting": The vault was opened with a key that weighed a pound. "We had to crank the old door like you now crank a Ford," longtime employee Henry Schweitzgebel recalled in the early 1900s. "I had to twist and twist like everything to get the bolts to jingle."

The Kansas City Savings Association's president was James. B. Bell, who held a substantial interest in the bank and had become its president in 1873. Bell left the bank in 1879 and sold his stake to W. A. Powell, who became president; Powell's son, A. H. Powell, assumed the presidency later that year. Francis Reid Long died in 1881. Interestingly, it was Bell's son Victor, along with Long's cousin Robert, who would (with a loan from the bank) soon establish the Long-Bell Lumber Company, which by the 1920s was the largest lumber company in the United States.

DR. WOODS: VISIONARY GENIUS

It took an entrepreneur, trained as a doctor, to transform the Kansas City Savings Association into a modern-day financial institution. That would be Dr. W. S. Woods.

William Stone Woods was born in Columbia, Missouri, in 1840. He was reared by his grandparents (his father, James Harris Woods, died when William was five years old). After graduating from the University of Missouri in 1861, he attended the Jefferson Medical College in Philadelphia and practiced medicine in Middle Grove and Paris, Missouri, both in Monroe County. In 1866, he married Albina McBride, daughter of a Monroe County judge.

Woods started a general merchandising business in Paris in 1867 and a year later, with his brother, James Moses Woods, began operating a wholesale grocery business that sold food and supplies to workers building the Union Pacific Railroad. The operation moved westward as construction of the railroad progressed from Omaha, Nebraska, toward Ogden, Utah, serving railroad builders as well as itinerant hangers-on whose dubious conduct provided the nickname of "Hell on Wheels" for many of the temporary boomtowns that sprouted along the route.

Woods returned to central Missouri in 1869 and settled in the Missouri River town of Rocheport, about 15 miles west of his native Columbia. There, he started his first bank, the Rocheport Savings Bank, capitalized by profits from his provisioning business. The bank struggled at first in the small town. Woods later noted that the storeowners had never used a bank and initially didn't want to put their money in his institution. "They were my enemies," he wrote, "and they discouraged the farmers from doing business with me. More than this, I had very little local support, and yet I remained there for some twelve years, built up a fine business and made a small fortune."

The town of Rocheport began to decline, however, as trade moved off the Missouri River and onto the new network of railroads. In 1881, Woods sold the bank and moved to Kansas City to become a partner in a dry goods store known as Grimes, Woods, LaForce & Company, which became the city's largest seller of textiles, clothing and personal-care supplies. Six months after his arrival in Kansas City, Woods purchased W. A. Powell's controlling interest in the Kansas City Savings Association and, as its president, immediately began a general overhaul of operations— shaping the culture that led the bank to its early success and that still distinguishes it to this day.

Woods was, as a contemporary noted, "a man of broad capabilities [who] has interested himself in other enterprises, comprehensive in their scope." In addition to running the bank, he retained an ownership stake in the dry goods store (which changed its name to Swofford Brothers under new majority ownership) and partnered with his brother James in a Dakota Territory cattle business that sold beef to

Dr. Woods led Commerce for 28 years, culminating in a rescue of the bank after the Panic of 1907. His actions typified those of the generation of American investors, boosters and entrepreneurs who developed the West: he established the predecessor of today's Commerce Bank and invested in a variety of other banks, real estate and businesses. He created a network of distant affiliated and correspondent banks that had connections to the Kansas City institution he was building at home. Woods was also an influential donor to the community, quietly contributing to a variety of charitable causes.

The Long-Bell Lumber Company

The rapid growth of the American West that began in the late 19th century required lumber to build railroads, homes and stores. One of the companies that provided that wood was the Long-Bell Lumber Company, which got its start in 1875 with an $8,000 loan from the Kansas City Savings Association, a precursor to Commerce Bank.

The bank and Long-Bell had close relationships. John W. Bell, who became president of the Kansas City Savings Association in 1873, was the father of Victor Bell, one of the founders of Long-Bell Lumber. Victor Bell's cousin, Robert A. Long, was also a Long-Bell founder, and his uncle, C. J. White, was the bank's cashier. Long was a cousin of Francis Reid Long, one of three founders of the bank, and White's son Robert was also a lumber company founder.

Long-Bell Lumber's origins date to 1874 when Robert Long, Victor Bell and Robert White went to Columbus, Kansas, to start a hay business. The young men were unsuccessful, but they discovered that the lumber used to build their sheds was more valuable than the hay. They tore down the sheds, sold the wood and opened a lumber business called R. A. Long & Company; its first shipment was unloaded on April 30,

1875. By 1883, the company owned 14 lumberyards throughout the Southwest. It changed its name to the Long-Bell Lumber Company, incorporated and moved to Kansas City in 1884.

In a 1928 letter, Robert Long remembered how Dr. William S. Woods, who took over the bank after the death of Francis Reid Long in 1881, provided Long-Bell Lumber with a line of credit to keep growing:

I went to the Doctor one day, told him we wanted a certain amount of money and suggested we might have some understanding as to how extensively the bank was willing to lend us. He replied, "Bob, you continue to send down your paper until I tell you to stop, and I don't think I shall ever make such a requirement of you." Having continued our connection with the institution as long as we have indicates, of course, the fair treatment we have received at its hands and accounts for my personally being ... one of its strongest friends and advocates.

Long-Bell became the largest lumber company in the United States in the 1920s. It was acquired by International Paper Company in 1956.

The intertwining of the Long and Bell families played a major role in the early development of Kansas City and helped create the largest lumber company in the United States during the expansive 1920s. The Long-Bell Lumber Company, co-founded by Francis Long's nephew Robert and funded in part by Commerce, provided the lumber to develop western communities and businesses. Top, a picnic hosted in 1925 by Mr. and Mrs. R. A. Long and Mr. and Mrs. R. P. Combs at the family's Longview Farm. Above, a Long-Bell Lumber logging camp in Tennant, California.

government forts and Indian agency offices. He also owned a number of valuable commercial buildings in Kansas City and became involved in charity work, especially education. Woods' legacy includes personally educating and providing opportunities for many young men who later became prominent Kansas City–area businessmen.

In 1882, not long after taking over leadership of the bank, Woods changed the bank's name to Bank of Commerce, accentuating its focus as a lender to businesses as well as individuals—with increased capital of $200,000. Three years later, marking the bank's 20th anniversary, he commissioned construction of a new banking house at Sixth and Delaware. According to a 1928 history of Commerce Bank, the new offices opened in "one of the finest buildings west of St. Louis."

The late 1800s was the golden era of "town boosters" who encouraged Americans to speculate on the growth of cities in the West. Woods was one of the strong advocates for the city, and he used the bank to further those efforts. He had the foresight to anticipate that a bank such as Commerce could support development and economic growth throughout its region.

When the Bank of Commerce took its national charter in 1887, it reorganized as the National Bank of Commerce. Bank of Commerce stockholders received three dollars for every dollar they had invested, and the bank continued to grow under Woods' leadership and his personal and careful approach to finance. As Dr. Woods wrote to a nephew whom he had sponsored in starting a Colorado bank:

I always make it a point to find out a man's resources from which he could make payment at maturity, and then you can always judge for yourself of his reliability. The fact is most banks make enough money if they keep out of bad debts, and as I said to you by word of mouth, I will forgive you for almost anything but bad debts.

In this remarkable letter to a young man starting his banking career, Woods explained his lending approach and philosophy, both of which remain essentially intact more than 125 years later, having served Commerce Bank well in good times and bad:

On the question of loans, never allow yourself to be hurried. Always talk with the man, get all you can out of him and learn all you can about the situation; consult the credit book which I shall send to you, and unless you are fully satisfied in the matter, say to him "Call tomorrow" or "this afternoon." Of course, if everything is favorable and there is no question of delay, it is well enough to say "yes." Say it cheerfully and pleasantly, and make him feel that you have done so with a good will, that gains good feeling on his part; but when there is a possibility of doubt, take the benefit of the doubt, and have him call tomorrow.

As Woods set out to expand his banking operation, Missouri laws prohibited him from opening other National Bank of Commerce locations in the state. He therefore purchased a string of banks in the adjacent state of Kansas: first, the Elk City Bank in Montgomery County and later, others in Medicine Lodge and Garnett.

Commerce was also a "banker's bank," and Woods garnered enduring goodwill by helping other banks in critical times. In 1890, for example, the National Bank of Commerce rescued a bank in Newton, Kansas, from insolvency by advancing it currency. With the money, Woods sent a note: "Order more as your needs require, as we propose to see you through." Three years later, the Newton bank returned the favor after deposits at the National Bank of Commerce fell significantly during one of the era's occasional panics: it kept its deposits in the National Bank of Commerce as a show of support. "In

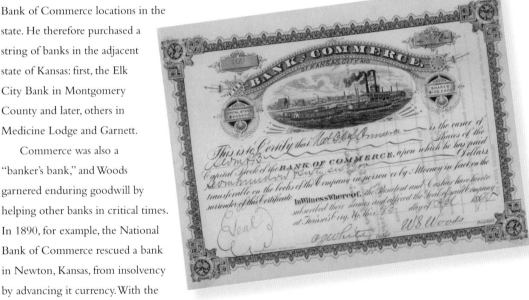

A document certifying the National Bank of Commerce's ownership of stock, below, reads: "This is to certify that Nat. Bk of Commerce is the owner of Seventy3 shares of the Capital Stock of the Bank of Commerce, upon which he has paid Seven hundred sixty-six dollars." It is dated April, 23, 1885, and signed by cashier A. G. White and president W. S. Woods.

1890, you came to our rescue," the Newton bank president wrote. "Without your help we would have closed, so we decided we could now stick with you and stand or fall with the Commerce."

STICKING WITH CUSTOMERS

Woods also stuck by his customers, some of whom were the leading regional entrepreneurs of the period. They included Arthur Stilwell, who organized more than 40 companies. In 1887, Stilwell founded what would become the Kansas City Southern Railway Company and built that railroad from Kansas City to the Gulf of Mexico at Port Arthur, Texas, (a town that he also established and named for himself). When Stilwell lost control of the Kansas City Southern in 1899, he proposed a new railway—the Kansas City, Mexico and Orient—from Kansas City to the Pacific Coast through Mexico. The National Bank of Commerce helped finance "The Orient."

In 1898, the bank moved again, opening a new headquarters at the corner of Tenth and Walnut streets in the city's former Journal Building, which Commerce had purchased and remodeled. By 1900, National Bank of Commerce was the largest bank west of Chicago, with deposits of $36 million. That same year, Woods and his nephew, Charles Quarles Chandler, bought the Kansas National Bank in Wichita. Within three years, Woods and his partners controlled 18 banks from Humboldt, Kansas, to Clayton, New Mexico—their principal objective being to serve the Southwest's huge and growing cattle business.

At the turn of the century, Kansas City had become the 22nd largest city in the United States, with a population of 163,000. A Missouri bank with a national charter was prohibited from opening branches, essentially to prevent banking concentration in the cities. To overcome that barrier and expand the business in parallel with the city's growth, Woods started the Commerce Trust Company, with himself as president. He appointed William Thornton ("W. T.") Kemper as vice president. Commerce Trust

WALNUT ST., NORTH FROM 12TH ST., BY NIGHT KANSAS CITY. MO.

opened on October 1, 1906, with four employees.

In addition to successfully running the Commerce Trust Company operation for 11 years, Kemper would go on to lead the entire bank at several critical turning points—notably during two changes of ownership in the late 1910s and early 1920s and through the Great Depression.

Kemper was born in the northwest Missouri town of Gallatin in 1865. By 1870, he had moved west with his family to near St. Joseph. At the age of 14, he began sweeping the floor of a St. Joseph shoe store in which his father was a partner; Kemper later became a shoe salesman there. By the 1880s, he owned his own store and had moved to Valley Falls, Kansas, where he became cashier in the bank run by Rufus Henry Crosby, an early Kansas pioneer and leader. W.T. married Crosby's daughter Charlotte in 1890 and became a partner in the bank in 1891, but when Crosby died later that year, the management of the bank was taken over by other relatives.

Like Dr. Woods before him, Kemper saw a promising future in Kansas City. He moved his family there in 1893 and organized the Kemper Mill and Elevator Company, which traded grain; the Kemper Investment Company; and the Kemper Mercantile Company, a mail-order business.

After 1885, the National Bank of Commerce was located at 545 Delaware, opposite; it moved to a building at Tenth and Delaware in 1898. The Commerce Trust Building, above, was completed in 1908. Right, a coin bank replica of the building was a promotional item given away to customers.

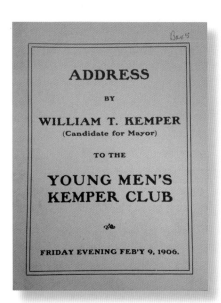

William Thornton Kemper, opposite, became the driving force at the new Commerce Trust Company after being hired by Dr. Woods to become its president in 1907. Well-connected and well-liked throughout Kansas City, he was known for greeting customers in the lobby and chatting with them about their lives and businesses. Kemper had a lifelong interest in politics and twice ran (unsuccessfully) for Kansas City mayor. Above is the cover of a published speech he gave to the Kansas City Young Men's Club during his 1906 campaign. The inkwell, right, from the early 1900s, offered customers this prudent advice: "Don't Spend It All."

He was elected to head the Board of Trade in 1898 at the age of 31, becoming its youngest president. W.T. ran twice (unsuccessfully) for mayor of Kansas City, in 1904 and again in 1906. While he maintained a lifelong interest and involvement in politics, he later said that losing those elections was the best thing that ever happened to him.

Woods prided himself on his ability to judge human nature, and he watched as Kemper grew his businesses. Believing Kemper could do for the bank what he'd done for his own companies, Woods invited Kemper to run the new Commerce Trust Company in 1906. His hunch was right: Kemper's personality, extensive network of connections and savvy understanding of how businesses worked was just what Commerce needed.

A "MAN'S MAN," GREETING CUSTOMERS IN THE LOBBY

Woods and Kemper complemented one another well. Both in business and philanthropy, Woods preferred to remain behind the scenes, seeking little attention for his work while paying strict attention to the financial details. W.T. Kemper, on the other hand, knew everyone in Kansas City, enjoyed talking to them whenever they came into the bank's offices and became the face of the bank.

Kemper completed his paperwork by 10 o'clock every morning so he could spend the rest of the day in the lobby, greeting customers. It was his way of keeping track of the community's goings-on and gaining intelligence about the market; his sociable manner imprinted the bank with a friendly personality and a reputation for service.

"People came into the bank to do their business, but also to talk to people," said James M. Kemper, Jr., W.T.'s grandson. "He was a man's man. He knew how to remember people's names." Indeed, W.T. Kemper made it a practice to call customers by their first names, and he welcomed requests for personal meetings. About evaluating customers, he said, "Find out what a man's made of. A person's character means more than his financial statement."

By the first decade of the 20th century, Kansas City had become a much more civilized place than the one the Longs had discovered on their arrival. Electric lights illuminated the interiors of stores downtown and were soon to be installed on the streets. Cable cars supplanted mule carts. The Democratic Party held its national convention in 1900 at the Kansas City Convention Hall, substantially raising the city's national profile.

In 1906, Woods announced that the bank, by now a major lender to the region's many grain and milling companies, would build a new 15-story headquarters at the corner of Tenth and Walnut (the former Journal Building was to be demolished). The new Commerce Building opened in 1908, housing both the National Bank of Commerce and the Commerce Trust Company, joined by an elegant marble staircase. Commerce Trust occupied the Tenth Street lobby and the National Bank of Commerce the Walnut lobby. The *Kansas City Post* wrote that the building was Kansas City's "largest and most up-to-date as well as handsomest office building" and that "it practically takes the place of a monument to the financial achievements of Dr. W. S. Woods."

"SOME PEOPLE MAY LEARN ECONOMY"

An unprecedented amount of wealth was created in the United States around the turn of the 20th century as the country continued to push westward. Rivers and mountains were crossed and the coasts connected by rail. Electricity and telephone communication fueled the rise of large regional and national-scale industries: railroads; iron, steel and coal production; utilities; manufacturing; agriculture. The country's net worth of

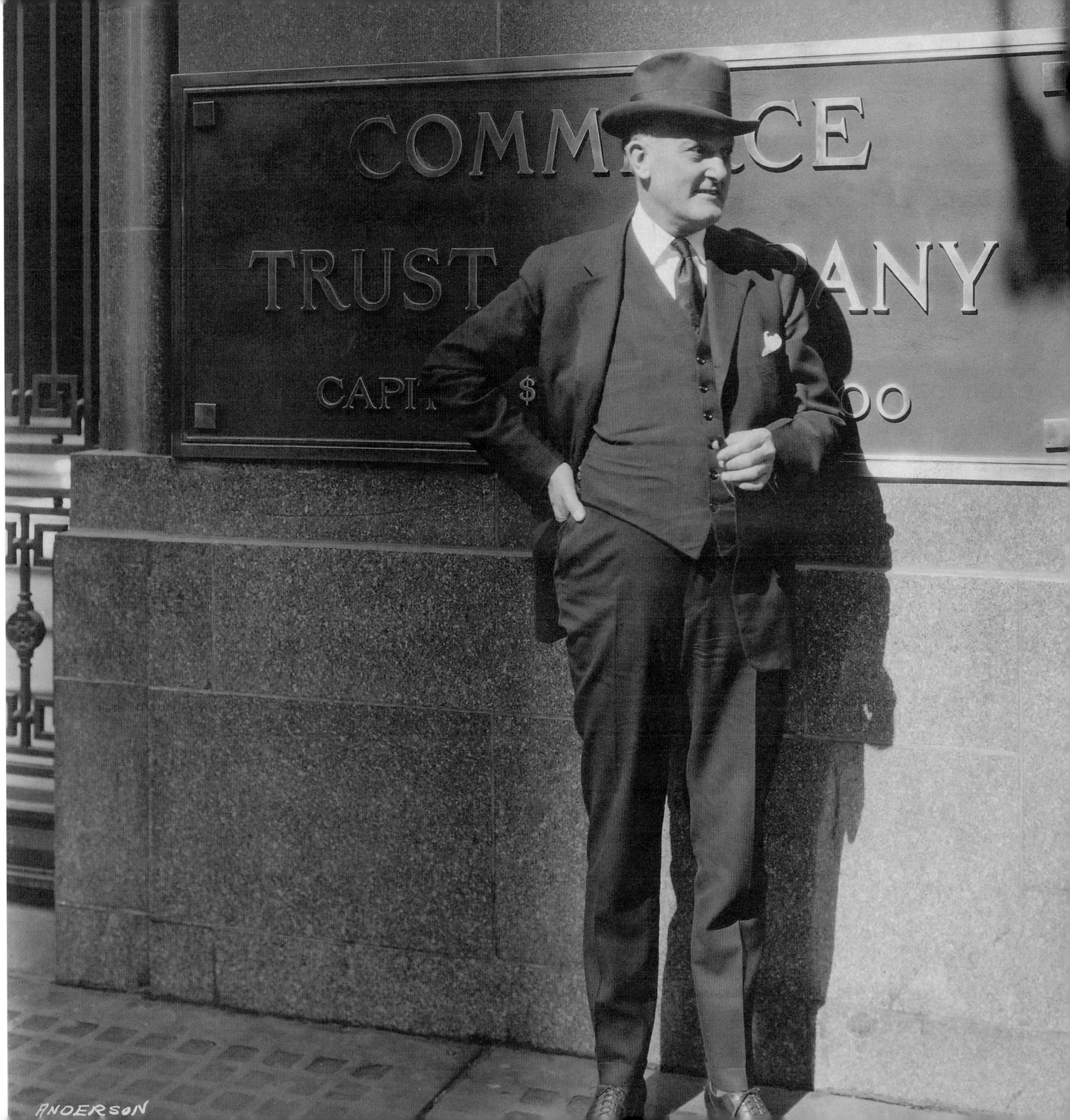
TRUST
ANDERSON

$43 billion in 1880 more than doubled to $107 billion by 1904, according to U.S. Census figures.

For banks, this increase in wealth added demand for a new service—managing families' money—to their core business of facilitating payments, capitalizing companies, providing credit and taking deposits. But there was an ominous side to the great abundance of wealth and the expanding opportunities in banking: many of the newly rich Americans started banks or financial institutions of their own and began providing credit for what were often later found to be unsuccessful operations.

Regionally, the West had a longstanding concern about the dominance of Eastern and European interests in control of the nation's supply of money and credit. The Democratic Party, led by Nebraskan William Jennings Bryan, had made this a major issue in its unsuccessful 1896 presidential campaign, a reflection of the tight-money/tight-credit conspiracy that Westerners saw in the nation's gold reserves–based monetary system.

Many Midwesterners felt Eastern banks didn't understand their way of life or the importance of farms to the economy and were therefore unwilling to provide the financial resources needed to support their growing economies. Midwestern banks, in turn, often claimed that the Eastern banks, which controlled the nation's money supply in the days before the Federal Reserve, deliberately didn't provide them with the liquidity they needed to serve their customers. Midwestern banks therefore took it upon themselves to promote the region, and they always encouraged the local businesses to use them—not only for the quality of their services, but for their mutual support.

In short, the approach to currency and banking at the turn of the century created a highly unstable economic environment in the United States. An 1893 panic, brought

about by speculation in railroads, was the worst depression the country had seen to that date, resulting in the failure of 150,000 businesses and the closure of some 500 banks—and another major banking crisis was right around the corner. The Panic of 1907 began with a failed attempt to corner the stock of United Copper Company. The move caused a cascade of events that resulted in a recession and a run on banks in several major cities in October and November.

Rumors spread that the National Bank of Commerce was overextended. Woods assured the U.S. Comptroller of the Currency, William Ridgely, that the bank would be able to withstand any demands by its depositors, who had decreased their account balances from more than $35 million to $12 million. Woods told the *Kansas City Star*, "Nobody is going to suffer. Some people may learn economy, but it will do them good."

Disagreeing with Woods' assessment of the bank's condition, Ridgely closed the National Bank of Commerce in December 1907, citing the heavy withdrawals as the reason. Woods sat in a room at the rear of the bank on the day of the closure and reassured customers by phone. "No, don't be uneasy," he said to one. "You haven't got a great city pounding, pounding night and day on you. We'll pay out; the collateral is good."

Woods convinced merchants in Kansas City to pay as much as they could on their outstanding loans so he could give money to depositors bent on closing their accounts. The bank also sold at a discount some of the railroad bonds it held in its portfolio to meet the demands of depositors. Woods issued a statement:

> *We hope to be able to open again in the near future, for business. We do not believe it is possible for a depositor in the National Bank of Commerce to lose a dollar. We beg your indulgence and forbearance until our affairs can be arranged to the satisfaction of all interested parties. We appreciate sensibly the confidence our numerous customers, large and small, have placed in us.*

A Future President

One of Commerce's early employees was future U.S. President Harry Truman. Born and raised in western Missouri, Truman was a couple of weeks shy of his 19th birthday when he applied for work at the bank on April 24, 1903. On his employment application, he stated that "theaters and reading" were his principal forms of recreation and that he typically spent his evenings and Sundays "at home." Asked if he had any extravagant tastes or habits, he wrote, "Don't think so."

Two family friends submitted letters attesting to his good character. When asked, "Are you good at figures?" Truman responded, "Fair." Asked if he had ever been suspended or expelled from school, Truman wrote, "No." Hired as a clerk, Truman was soon put in charge of the filing vault for a salary of $20 per month.

Periodically, a senior official at the bank, Charles H. Moore, asked Truman's supervisor, A. D. Flintom, for an evaluation of Truman's progress. "Truman … is an exceptionally bright young man and is keeping the work up in the vault better than it has ever been kept," Flintom reported to Moore on April 14, 1904. "We never had a boy in the vault like him before. He watches everything very closely and by his watchfulness, detects many errors which a careless boy would let slip through. His appearance is good and his habits and character are of the best." Flintom amplified his praise in his report of September 28, 1904: "I do not know of a better young man in the bank."

Truman's brother, John Vivian Truman, also worked at Commerce, but the boys quit on March 15, 1905, to help their parents move from Kansas City to a farm near Clinton, Missouri. On April 3, 1905, Harry Truman again applied for employment at the bank—and again mentioned that he was "fair" with figures—and was promptly rehired. He quit again six weeks later to take a job at nearby Union National Bank.

His housemate during his time at Commerce was a young Arthur Eisenhower, brother of future war hero and President Dwight D. Eisenhower. Arthur Eisenhower worked for the bank for 50 years, rising to the position of chief credit officer.

Commerce's early employees included Harry S. Truman, the future U.S. president, above, and Arthur Eisenhower, brother of President Dwight D. Eisenhower. Truman's tenure at the bank was relatively short-lived; Eisenhower worked at Commerce for more than 50 years, becoming chief credit officer. The two lived in the same boarding house during Truman's tenure at the bank. Left, Truman's Commerce job application from 1903.

The pace of events was too much for the bank, however, and Woods was unable to stay ahead of the rumors, which eroded public confidence. As comptroller, Ridgely suspended the bank's ownership and placed the bank in receivership, pending reorganization. He then resigned his official position in Washington and moved to Kansas City, where in March 1908 he appeared as president of the reopened bank. Woods was retained as a director.

Ridgely and his brother, Edward, who was installed as cashier, forced Woods to take personal ownership of certain bank-owned assets that the Ridgelys thought worthless. Ironically, these subsequently became very valuable to Woods. All of this took place before the days of the Securities and Exchange Commission and the Federal Reserve System.

The Ridgelys' takeover was short-lived, as the brothers underestimated the loyalty that the Kansas City community and other banks felt for Woods. Woods and his associates quietly bought shares of the bank's stock. By November, they had accumulated nearly 13,000 of the bank's 20,000 shares, regained control of the bank and forced the Ridgely brothers to resign. The Ridgelys moved back East, and there is no record that they were ever seen again in Kansas City.

A QUICK TURNAROUND

By the time Woods was back in control of the bank, the panic had subsided, and the National Bank of Commerce made good on its promise to its customers. None of them lost a penny. One customer, the Citizens Bank of Abilene, Kansas, decided to keep its money in the bank even after it was temporarily closed. The bank's chairman, Mike Malott, wrote in a letter, "We had several opportunities to assign this account at a slight discount, but our directors said this, 'We have had three basic failures in Abilene, and in each instance Commerce wired us to order all the currency we might possibly need.'"

Its management restored, the National Bank of Commerce regained depositors and business customers,

Customers stand outside Commerce Trust Company's safe deposit vault around 1908. Investors deposited securities in these vaults and would need to visit regularly to clip the coupons that were attached to bonds as they matured for collection by the bank. The sign on the desk at left reads, "I.W. Lively, Manager, Safe Deposit Vaults."

validating its practice of being there for its customers and community when they were in need. Commerce proved that it could survive when other banks couldn't, largely because of the relationships it had built.

Woods' National Bank of Commerce had been tried and proven to have been on solid financial ground all along, and by the end of 1908, deposits rose to $27 million, an increase of $15 million in just nine months. The bank purchased Union National Bank in November that year, and some executives of that bank left to form another bank in Kansas City, Southwest National Bank. Union National's president, D. T. Beals, became president of the National Bank of Commerce in the transaction. Beals soon fell ill, however, and the board elected J. W. Perry to succeed him.

Poor health forced Woods to retire in the spring of 1909. Although he and his wife moved to California and spent most of their time there, they always considered Kansas City their home—and Woods, still a large stockholder, kept in close touch with the bank's goings-on. In fact, he protested vociferously when, in January 1912, the bank changed its

name to Southwest National Bank of Commerce after acquiring Southwest National Bank and adopting a new name that blended those of the previous institutions. F. P. Neal, one of the officers who had left Union National to form Southwest, became chairman of the board of the merged banks. Perry was president, and Kemper remained head of the Commerce Trust Company.

The great economic expansion of the Midwest in the latter half of the 19th century had helped Commerce grow into the largest financial institution between San Francisco and St. Louis. Challenging economic conditions would face the bank again in the decades to come, but Commerce would overcome them all, largely because of the traditions set by Woods' connection to the community and the tone he had set in the way his bank would be run.

As bank President J. W. Perry later reflected, looking back on the events by which Woods and his colleagues put Commerce back in local hands: "The stockholders feel that the bank has passed beyond private ownership and is now a part of the community that made it."

During the Panic of 1907, the Comptroller of the Currency, William Ridgely, above, left office to form a group that seized control of Commerce. Ridgely was removed as head of the bank the following year when Woods and his associates regained control and recapitalized the bank. Commerce added "Southwest" to its name in 1912 following the acquisition of a rival banking company.

Southwest National Bank of Commerce

Commerce Trust Company

MEMBERS FEDERAL RESERVE SYSTEM

Capital, Surplus and Profits .. $ 5,929,936
Deposits 52,066,977
Total Resources 62,218,511

Capital, Surplus and Profits .. $ 2,319,215
Deposits 29,772,047
Total Resources 31,956,568

Combined Capital, Surplus and Profits . . . . $ 8,249,151
Combined Deposits 81,839,024
Combined Total Resources. 94,175,079

A newspaper advertisement, left, showed the combined strength of the banks and listed their numerous directors and officers. The bank lobby was bustling with activity for much of the time, as shown in the photo opposite.

DIRECTORS.

Jas. T. Bradley, R. A. Long,
R. P. Brewer, W. S. McLucas,
G. S. Carkener, F. P. Neal,
F. G. Crowell, J. C. Nichols,
W. S. Dickey, E. D. Nims,
Bruce Dodson, J. W. Perry,
Edward George, A. W. Peet,
John G. Groves, W. A. Pickering,
H. A. Guettel, F. G. Robinson,
J. D. Guyton, C. J. Schmelzer,
W. E. Halsell, O. C. Snider,
S. Harzfeld, H. Vanderslice,
J. J. Heim, S. H. Velie,
Geo. R. Hicks, C. H. Whitehead,
[illegible] F. D. Whiting,
F. W. Zea.

OFFICERS.

W. T. KEMPER, Chairman of Boards.
J. W. PERRY, President.
R. P. BREWER, Vice-President.
JAS. T. BRADLEY, Vice-President and Cashier.
C. M. VINING, Assistant Cashier.
H. Y. LEMON, Assistant Cashier.
FRANK C. MITCHELL, Assistant Cashier.
W. H. GLASKIN, Assistant Cashier.
E. P. WHEAT, Assistant Cashier.
A. B. EISENHOWER, Assistant Cashier.

C. S. McLUCAS, President.
RICHAR C. MENEFEE, Vice-Pres.
DWNLEY CULBERTSON, Vice-President.
C. C. SCHWITZGEBEL, Secretary.
O ZACH MILLER III, Treasurer.
GEORGE H. HUDDY, Asst. Sec'y.
EORGE W. DILLON, Ass't. Sec'y.
W. ROSS, Ass't Sec'y.
C. HOWARD, Trust Officer.
ERALD PARKER, Mgr. Bond Department.
M. STAKER, Mgr. Safe Deposit Vaults.
SANFORD MILLER, Mgr. Saving Department.
MES J. SWOFFORD, JR., Mgr. New Business Department.

DIRECTORS.

F. J. Bannister, W. F. Helm,
Gordon T. Beaham, John Kelley,
W. T. Bland, W. T. Kemper,
C. A. Braley, R. A. Long,
F. D. Crabbs, W. S. McLucas,
W. S. Dickey, R. C. Menefee,
E. Dickinson, John R. Mulvane,
Geo. H. Edwards, J. C. Nichols,
U. S. Epperson, Louis Oppenstein,
Chas. E. Faeth, J. W. Perry,
L. H. Fisher, Elijah Robinson,
J. D. Guyton, F. G. Robinson,
D. J. Haff, W. A. Rule,
W. E. Halsell, T. M. Walker,
W. S. Woods,

Commerce Trust employees posed with Dr. Woods, first row, left, for a portrait in the bank's lobby around 1913. Opposite, a 15-year employee service pin from Commerce Trust features the logo the bank used in the early 1900s.

TRADITIONS AND VALUES

The Panic of 1907 raised concerns about the banking industry's capacity to withstand liquidity problems, and in response, the government began discussions that would lead to a new regulatory system. U.S. Senator Robert L. Owen from the new state of Oklahoma and others in Congress proposed creating a "central bank" that would control the nation's money supply and regulate so-called "member" banks that were not federally chartered. Comprising a network of 12 district banks that would be owned by the member banks and operate locally with oversight from a board of governors in Washington, D.C., the Federal Reserve System was created in December 1913 with President Woodrow Wilson's signature.

Cities across the United States campaigned to host one of the regional Federal Reserve banks, recognizing that the presence of such a bank would elevate the stature of their business communities and help them grow. New York, Chicago, Pittsburgh, Boston and St. Louis were obvious choices because of their prominence in the country's economy. Because many thought the government would never place two Federal Reserve banks in the same state, Kansas City was viewed as a long shot.

Commerce was influential in the institution and organization of the Federal Reserve Bank of Kansas City; the Kansas City Fed held its first meeting in the Commerce boardroom in 1914. This photo shows an early meeting of the district bank's organizing committee that year. At far left is Jo Zach Miller, a Commerce executive who would later become the Fed bank's first president. Opposite, an early Commerce Trust savings passbook offered tips to customers to manage their finances responsibly.

A.E. RAMSEY

W. J. BAILEY.

"I THINK IT DEMANDS IT"

William T. Kemper and other executives of Commerce believed otherwise. They reasoned that, although Kansas City was not among the top U.S. cities in terms of capital and surplus held in its national banks, Commerce was a major conduit for other banks throughout the growing Southwest. To have a Federal Reserve Bank in Kansas City would recognize the importance of the region and confirm that the city was indeed a major financial center.

Treasury Secretary William McAdoo, head of the government's Reserve Bank Organization Committee, held hearings across the country at which bankers and businessmen argued why their cities should get Federal Reserve banks. The hearing in Kansas City took place on January 23, 1914, exactly one month after Wilson signed the Federal Reserve Act. At the hearing, McAdoo was presented with a proposal for a Federal Reserve district—to include Kansas, Nebraska, Oklahoma, New Mexico and parts of Missouri and Colorado—that would be based in Kansas City. The district would encompass more than 1,300 national banks, or 18 percent of the country's total.

Kansas City at the time ranked seventh in the country in terms of the value of checks cleared, and Southwest National Bank of Commerce was the city's largest clearinghouse bank. Furthermore, Kansas City was the world's largest wheat and hay market and it was No. 2, behind Chicago, in livestock transactions. Commerce Chairman F. P. Neal opined that such a vibrant, bustling city merited having a Federal Reserve Bank, not a branch.

"The business of Kansas City naturally … would be so large that it would be beyond the purview of a branch bank, because we think we have already shown you by statistics filed and by the statements made that a business naturally centers here that would be much more than you might expect any branch bank to undertake," Neal said. Asked by Secretary of Agriculture David Houston, another member of the committee, whether Neal was arguing that the volume of business in Kansas City justified a main Federal Reserve Bank, Neal replied, "I think it demands it."

The committee polled national banks in the proposed Tenth Federal Reserve District to learn where they thought the bank should be located. Kansas City received 355 first-place votes, followed by Omaha and Denver. When the committee announced its decision on April 2, 1914, it was clear that the city's lobbying efforts had paid off. The Federal Reserve Bank of Kansas City opened in November 1914, holding its first meeting in the Commerce boardroom.

Jo Zach Miller, Jr., who had come to Kansas City in 1910 to work as a vice president for Commerce Trust and was a protégé of W. T. Kemper, was chosen as chairman of the Kansas City Fed. To accept the position, Miller had to sell his stock in Commerce Trust and accept a salary of $7,500—less than what he had been making at the bank.

CHANGE AT THE TOP

As W. T. Kemper led Commerce Trust Company through the second decade of the 20th century, he groomed his elder two sons, Crosby and James, to become bankers. Both sons attended the University of Missouri, and their father wrote them regularly, every letter encouraging conservative spending and hard work.

1. How much money have I made this year? Answer
2. How much of it have I saved? Answer
3. Of that which I have spent, how much was for necessary living expenses? Answer
4. How much for legitimate, wholesome amusement? Answer
5. How much needlessly squandered? Answer
6. Will I always be happier for having spent the amount in question in No. 5? Answer
7. Am I proud of my answer to No. 2? Answer

SAVINGS DEPARTMENT
Commerce Trust Company
H AND WALNUT STS.   KANSAS CITY, MO.

THIS BOOK MUST BE PRESENTED WHEN MONEY
IS DEPOSITED OR WITHDRAWN

Kansas City's Union Station opened in 1914. The city's position as a rail center enabled the bank's check-processing business to grow dramatically. Commerce had workers at the train station to meet the trains as they arrived, then process and forward checks as "cash letters" for final payment.

In 1916, while W. T.'s sons were in college, Southwest National Bank of Commerce acquired the Commerce Trust Company, although by agreement, the companies operated with separate officers and boards of directors for five years after the acquisition. To facilitate an eventual consolidation, Kemper retired from Commerce Trust in early 1917, selling his 2,275 shares in the trust company for $325 per share. He was granted a $200,000 bonus, and he agreed not to become an officer in another bank for at least three years.

Kemper's retirement didn't last long. By July 1917, Commerce had convinced him to return as chairman of both boards of directors. His return to the bank coincidentally came less than a month after the death of his mentor and former boss, Dr. William Stone Woods, who passed away in June at the Elms Hotel in Excelsior Springs, Missouri, at the age of 76. The *Kansas City Star* noted in his obituary that Woods "would rather lend a million dollars on character than on a security." In reference to the Ridgely takeover and Woods' reacquisition of the bank roughly a decade earlier, the *Star* called Woods "a man with active enemies and active friends" and noted that "it was often said of him that his work was as old gold and that he never forgot his friends."

W. T.'s eldest son, Crosby, meanwhile, graduated from Missouri and spent a year at the Wharton School in Philadelphia, studying banking before returning to Kansas City. He worked briefly at Commerce Trust before his father put him to work at Kemper Mill and Elevator.

After World War I, W. T. put his younger son, James, in charge of City Center Bank (a predecessor to UMB Financial), a small bank in Kansas City that he personally had acquired in April 1918. But James, who had trained as a bookkeeper at the Oklahoma State Bank in Enid, Oklahoma (also owned by his father), resigned a month after taking over so he could bring his wife, Gladys Woods Grissom (who coincidentally was Dr. Woods' granddaughter) to live in California for health reasons. Crosby was then installed as the president of City Center Bank.

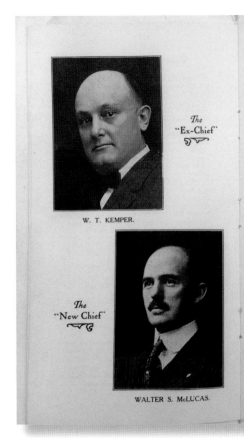

The "Ex-Chief"
W. T. KEMPER.

The "New Chief"
WALTER S. McLUCAS.

In 1919, Commerce dropped the word "Southwest" from its corporate title and reverted to its previous name, National Bank of Commerce. The final consolidation of National Bank of Commerce and Commerce Trust Company took place in March 1921, and a single company was established, taking the name Commerce Trust Company—with W. T. Kemper as chairman and J. W. Perry as president. Walter S. McLucas, who had been president of Commerce Trust since just before Kemper's 1917 "retirement," departed to take a position as vice president with a large bank in New York.

As they jointly led the consolidated bank in the first years of the 1920s, Kemper and Perry fell into disagreement on important management matters—and their inability to see eye to eye resulted in the sale of the bank. In October 1922, Kemper and Perry retired and sold their interests in

Commerce Comment kept employees apprised of what was going on at the company and with their co-workers. The February 1917 issue listed officers and other employees and included a "personals" section noting the promotions and departures of employees, the return of an employee from the war front and even the birth of bank executive Jo Zach Miller's son.

Commerce Trust to Theodore Gary and Associates, whose main business was operating telephone companies in the United States and overseas. The Gary interests brought Walter McLucas back to Commerce to run the bank as president. To preserve a connection with the Kemper family, Gary invited James Kemper to return from California and made him the bank's treasurer.

With his retirement from banking, W. T. Kemper turned the majority of his attention and his business acumen to the railroad industry. He had been appointed receiver of the Kansas City, Mexico & Orient Railroad in 1917 and had concluded that its existence was unsustainable given

a realistic projection of traffic. After World War I ended in 1918, Kemper obtained a $2.5 million government loan to improve operations. However, the railroad continued to operate at a deficit until oil was discovered along its route, near Big Lake, Texas, in May 1923. Traffic spiked and fees rose as the railroad was used to ship supplies into and oil out of the area, and by 1924 the railroad was operating at a profit.

The following year, Kemper and a business partner, Clifford Histed, bought control of the railroad for $3 million and immediately expanded its operations. Kemper took no salary for running the KCM&O between 1917 and 1927,

VR COMMERCE TRUST CO. AT MISSION HILLS CLUB 7/8/16

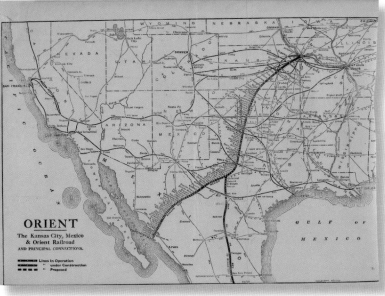

ORIENT
The Kansas City, Mexico
& Orient Railroad
AND PRINCIPAL CONNECTIONS.

Lines in Operation
"   "   under Construction
"   "   Proposed

Many have noted that high among Commerce's strengths are its employees at all levels; employee recognition and employee events have been an important part of the Commerce culture from the beginning. Above, employees gathered outside the Mission Hills Club (now the Carriage Club) on July 8, 1916, for the first annual Commerce Trust Company employee dinner. When W.T. Kemper retired (temporarily) from Commerce in 1922, he and a partner purchased control of the Kansas City, Mexico & Orient Railroad; at left, an Orient system map from 1921 shows its expansive network and ambitious plans.

The Women's Department

In 1921, a year after women gained the right to vote in the United States, W.T. Kemper wanted to make the bank more available to a previously untapped market. He created a Women's Department at Commerce Trust to make banking and personal finance more relevant to the bank's female customers.

The department's brochure stated, "Personal attention and assistance will be graciously and gladly given in opening accounts, handling checks and other matters which sometimes puzzle women."

Doris Beebe was put in charge of the department, and she did everything from answering daily requests to giving speeches about women in the business world. "People go to their doctor to talk about their aches and pains, to their minister to talk about their souls, and to their banks for these reasons plus every other reason on Earth—and sometimes for no reason at all," she

said. "This is especially true of women, for their banking business is to them more personal than commercial."

The attention to women also existed in the employee ranks. By the end of World War II, Commerce had become the first bank in Kansas City to name a woman as an executive. Emma Hall, an authority on government bonds, was named assistant vice president in 1945 and worked at the bank for 31 years.

The Women's Department at Commerce, which made a point of familiarizing women with the concepts of banking and financial management, was one of the first programs by any bank to address the needs of women in this regard. Doris Beebe, left, ran the Women's Department during the 1920s, when, as shown above, it could be a busy place.

and in 1928 he sold the railroad to the Atchison, Topeka &
Santa Fe Railroad for more than $8 million—reportedly
making a profit of more than $6 million.

THE TROUBLESHOOTER

During W.T. Kemper's absence from the bank's day-to-day
operations, Commerce Trust continued to grow. After his
father stepped away from management, James Kemper asked
McLucas for more responsibilities and was given the job
of working through problems the bank was having with its
loans to the W. S. Dickey Clay Manufacturing Company.
After spending weeks learning Dickey's business (and how
successful manufacturers operated), James offered a plan to
change the factory's operations. The plan was executed, and
soon the factory was making money and repaying its loan.

Now with a reputation as a troubleshooter, James
Kemper was named bank president in 1925 at the age of
31 (overcoming the objections of some board members who
felt he simply wasn't old enough).

"I suspect that people … had begun to recognize his
intelligence and steadfast courage," his son James Kemper, Jr.
would say later. "My father had a knack for concentrating
completely on the problem at hand and catching the main
point at issue, and he was always able to foresee threatening
clouds when the going was good."

INNOVATIONS IN TRANSIT AND CORRESPONDENT BANKING

Commerce grew its business in the 1920s on a foundation
of basic banking—taking deposits and making loans—and
creating new businesses out of an innovative approach to
managing funds and processing paperwork. For example, in
1923, at a time when transactions were entirely paper-based,
Commerce built a check processing system for itself and
other banks that could efficiently handle more than 500,000
checks a day; not only did this improve service to customers
and give Commerce a source of revenue, it brought the
bank new deposit customers when check-processing clients
kept accounts with the bank.

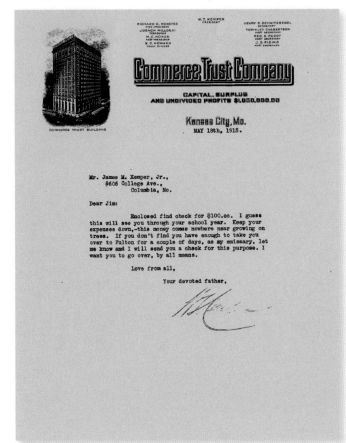

*W.T. Kemper, Jr., W.T.
Kemper, Sr., R. Crosby
Kemper, Sr., and James M.
Kemper, Sr., left to right, all
played prominent roles in
Kansas City banking in the
mid-1920s. A family story
holds that James Sr., the
youngest of this group, grew
his moustache to appear
older. W.T. Sr. dictated
letters, left, to be typed on
company stationery and
sent to his elder sons Crosby
and James while they were
students at the University
of Missouri in Columbia.
He consistently urged thrift
and hard work, among
other virtues.*

Five years later, Commerce began the first 24-hour banking transit department in the country. Bankers had forever struggled to identify and combat check kiters—people who would open bank accounts, write large checks and then cover their overdrafts with checks drawn on another bank by taking advantage of the lag time between when a check was written and when it was presented for collection. To speed up collection of checks, Commerce set up an operation at Kansas City's Union Station where workers would take checks off trains, immediately process them and put them on a waiting train for shipment to other banks, which would be able to post them against accounts the next morning. With Commerce's solution, the checks often reached the paying bank several days sooner than before. In later years, Commerce chartered a fleet of airplanes to deliver checks the next day.

Commerce also expanded its correspondent banking operations in the 1920s, serving small community banks that turned to bigger banks for assistance in making large business loans or providing other special services. By the early 1930s, Commerce ranked among the top correspondent banks in the country, and correspondent bankers who worked for Commerce sometimes kept packed suitcases at the office so they could leave immediately when a small bank called for help.

REACQUIRING THE BANK
Such practices benefited Commerce when the October 1929 stock market crash caused massive bank runs and led to the Great Depression. Commerce suffered losses, but it was not hurt as badly as banks that had loaned money to speculators in Florida real estate and on Wall Street—practices Commerce had deliberately avoided.

The terrible economic conditions did,

however, force Theodore Gary's company to reassess its ownership of the bank, and in late 1932, W. T. Kemper and son James reacquired Commerce for $86 a share—less than half of what they had sold it for a decade earlier. When Walter McLucas left the bank the following year to become president of the then troubled National Bank of Detroit, W. T. was again chairman of Commerce—his third time at the helm since 1917. Interestingly, A. P. Giannini, California's famous founder of Bank of America, bought a roughly 12.5 percent stake in the bank.

Franklin D. Roosevelt was elected as the country's president in 1932—W. T. Kemper, active in politics, went to Washington to hear the inaugural address the following March 4. Two days after his inauguration, Roosevelt called for a "banking holiday" to arrest a month-long run on American banks. Initially planned for only four days, the suspension of banking lasted for more than a week, and when the government allowed the first banks to reopen on March 13, Commerce Trust was among them, having been judged by the U.S. Treasury to be sound.

With unemployment reaching

Commerce's Transit Department, opposite, processed thousands of checks every day and helped grow the bank's prominence in the Midwest in the 1920s and the 1930s. Documenting this activity could be tedious and labor-intensive: every transaction had to be recorded by hand, as evidenced by the ledger, below, from the 1920s.

almost 25 percent and the stock market down nearly 70 percent from its 1929 high, people needed whatever funds they could get their hands on. Before the bank holiday, many of Commerce's customers had come to stand in line to make withdrawals. With his characteristic style, when he saw a lengthening line of waiting customers, W. T. Kemper sent some of his employees to the City Market to purchase apples, and he personally handed them out to people in line. After a few bites, some customers stepped out of line. Kemper's show of personal regard inspired mutual goodwill and confidence in his leadership in troubled times.

The 1930s were indeed hard on the nation. Unemployment exceeded 15 percent for virtually the entire decade. Commerce's performance reflected the country's pain but was less severe. This can be attributed in part to customers' confidence and loyalty, but also to the Kansas City community, which had undertaken significant public

works to keep the local economy from stagnating, and to the bank's underlying strength. Commerce had moved many illiquid assets into a separate corporate entity outside the bank, while leaving in place the financial capacity to meet its customers' needs and, in fact, launch a new phase of growth.

Of the 30,000 U.S. banks in existence just prior to the 1929 stock market crash, 9,000 failed during the Depression. Commerce not only recovered, it grew. By the end of 1933, deposits were $90 million—up from $59 million at the beginning of the year—and when Commerce celebrated its 70th anniversary in 1935, it had $150 million in deposits, an estimated 141,000 customers and 560 employees.

W. T. Kemper held the title of Commerce's chairman until his death in January 1938. His passing left son James to succeed W. T. and to carry forward a philosophy, strategy and customer-first culture that would guide the bank into the future.

Capital & Surplus __ 8 Million
Deposits _____ 150 Million
Total Resources __ 161 Million
Number of Customers 141 Thousand

The bank lobby was festooned with flowers, and a marching band played when Commerce celebrated its 70th anniversary in 1935. Opposite, W.T. Kemper, Sr., far left, and son James, second from right, met with longtime employees that year. Robert Keith is at center, and far right is L. E. Wassmer, who was celebrating 37 years with the bank. The identify of the man to W.T.'s left is unknown.

It was said that Commerce bankers would keep their bags packed in the office in case they needed to visit a correspondent banking partner at a moment's notice. Standing at the ready were James Kemper, Jr., fourth from left, and 10 other managers of Commerce Trust from the 1940s. Opposite, an employee pin symbolizes a new era of growth for Commerce, showcasing the clock installed on the Commerce Trust building in the 1950s.

DON'T TAKE THE RISKS YOU DON'T UNDERSTAND

Commerce Trust Company entered the 1940s on the rise. With more than $185 million in deposits, it ranked as the nation's 36th largest bank. But a war that had recently broken out in Europe was edging closer to U.S. shores, and its effect on the bank would soon be tragic in a deeply personal way.

Now in his mid-40s with two well-educated sons each around 20 years of age, James Kemper, Sr. recognized that it was time to bring the next generation into the family business, and he planned to groom sons David and James Jr. for positions at the bank in much the same way his father had done with him. Both sons had worked at the bank in the summers during college.

David had graduated from Harvard, where he majored in history and wrote his thesis on the farm credit system, and attended a year of graduate school at Stanford. He and James Jr., two years younger, worked in a variety of roles at the bank in the 1930s. War interrupted the Kempers' full initiation into banking, however, as they both enlisted in the United States Army in 1942. It was assumed that David, as the eldest sibling, would take over the top spot when his father was ready to step away from day-to-day business, but David was killed in action on April 25, 1945—just two weeks before fighting ended in Europe.

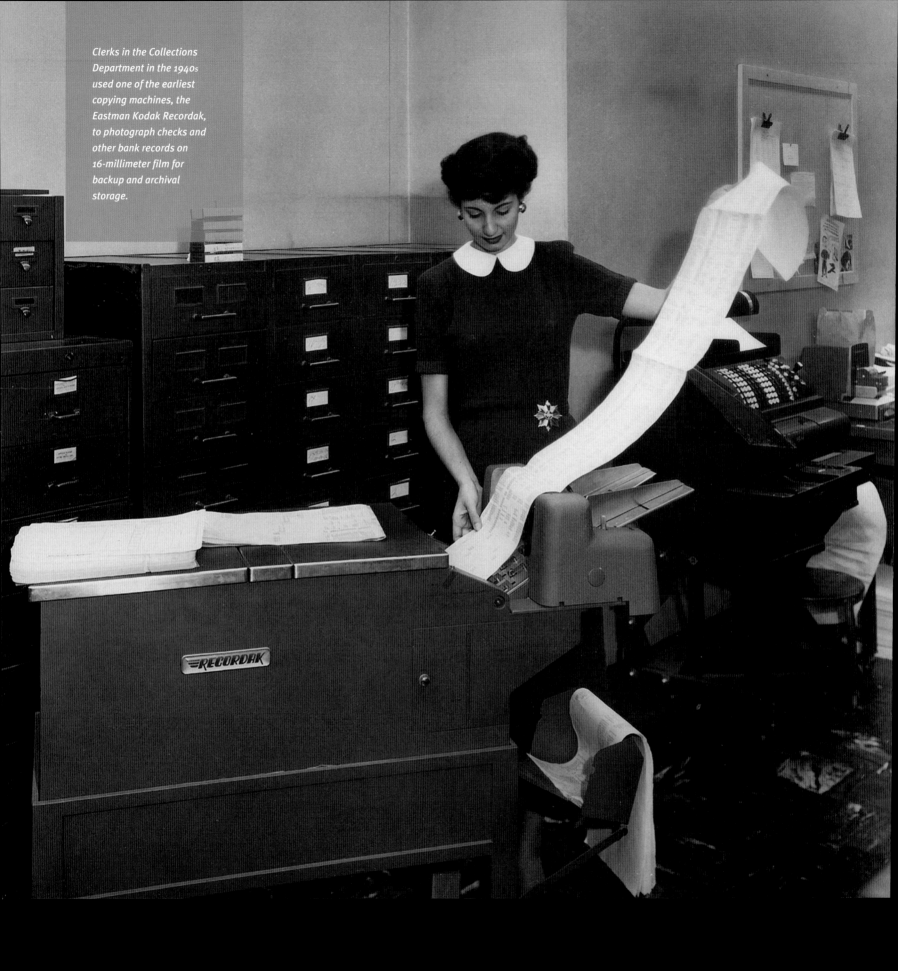

Clerks in the Collections Department in the 1940s used one of the earliest copying machines, the Eastman Kodak Recordak, to photograph checks and other bank records on 16-millimeter film for backup and archival storage.

THE WAR AND BEYOND

During the war years, James Kemper, Sr. continued to lead Commerce Trust to steady growth. In 1943, the bank's capital surplus grew to $14 million, up from $9 million a decade earlier. The following year, the bank opened a foreign department, which met with quick success by offering to transfer funds for bank customers to family members stationed overseas during the war.

In 1944, Commerce purchased A. P. Giannini's Commerce shares and distributed them to the bank's existing shareholders. It also declared a five-for-one stock split, with 60,000 shares at $100 apiece being reissued as 300,000 shares at $20 each. The next year, the company declared a 50 percent stock dividend.

James Jr. was discharged from the Army in November 1945. He completed his college studies and graduated from Yale with a degree in economics, then returned to Missouri to begin his banking training at the First National Bank of Independence, which was controlled by the family. On December 1, 1946, he moved to Commerce Trust, where he started work as an assistant cashier. Soon after that, he started courting his future wife: Mildred Lane, a librarian at the Federal Reserve Bank of Kansas City.

One of James Kemper, Sr.'s legacies is the team of professional managers he brought into Commerce—men who would go on to lead the bank in the 1950s and 1960s and who looked to him as a mentor. He was helped in that task by Arthur Eisenhower, President Dwight D.

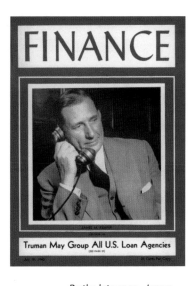

FINANCE

Truman May Group All U.S. Loan Agencies

By the late 1940s, James Kemper, Sr. was grooming his own sons for future leadership at the bank; David, left, and James sat with their sister Julianne and their stepmother, Eleanor Jones Kemper, for a 1935 portrait. James Kemper, Sr. was featured on the cover of the July 10, 1945, issue of Finance magazine in a two-page profile headlined, "Kemper Made His Own Way: Missouri Banker is Guided by Common-Sense Policies."

Commerce's leadership team in the mid-1950s included James Kemper, Jr., seated; Arthur Eisenhower, left; and Joseph Williams, Sr. At the time this photograph was taken in 1955, Williams was president of the bank, with Kemper soon to succeed him, and Eisenhower was chief credit officer. Commerce was the first bank in Kansas City to name a woman as an executive— Emma Hall, right, an authority on government bonds who became an assistant vice president. Her distinguished career at the bank spanned more than three decades.

Eisenhower's brother, who had started at the bank under Dr. Woods and was now its chief credit officer. Arthur Eisenhower would work at Commerce for more than 50 years before retiring in the 1950s.

With the end of World War II came a decade of economic expansion in the United States, and Kemper and his team at Commerce played an important role in the Midwest's postwar growth. The bank continued to grow, as well; in fact, its financial performance was such in 1947 that all employees received a bonus equaling 16 percent of their salaries. That same year, recognizing the need for consistent performance, Commerce implemented a training program to ensure that its workers had the skills they needed to serve customers well, thrive in their jobs and take the next steps in their careers.

NURTURING COMPANIES

James Kemper, Sr. relinquished his position as Commerce president in 1948 to Joseph C. Williams but remained as chairman. He kept an office on the third floor of the bank and continued to sit in on weekly senior loan meetings, making his feelings known on every application as he had for some two decades. As far as James Sr. was concerned, "The problem of lending money is simply a matter of deciding whether a man wants to pay you and whether he can."

James Kemper, Jr. explained his father this way: "People who were seeking to mislead and deceive the community could not have found a tougher banker to do business with, but even in the direst situations, people who sincerely needed help could look to him, not only for sound advice but also for positive action."

Eisenhower and the Kempers institutionalized Commerce's lending practices in the 1950s, a time when the U.S. economy was booming. With the economy growing at an annualized rate of 3.6 percent during the decade, consumer goods in great demand and business innovation at unprecedented levels, many companies that are household names today were established or achieved critical mass. A number of Commerce's Kansas City–based commercial

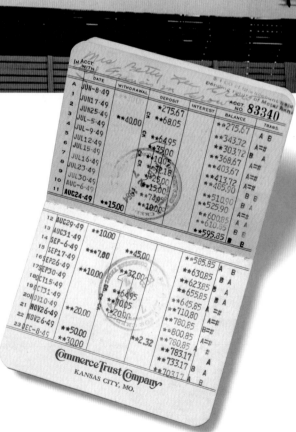

Commerce Trust employed a variety of marketing approaches during the 1950s. Billboards like the one above were often sighted around Kansas City. The popularity of television, meanwhile, offered new opportunities to tie in with one of the medium's new stars; in October 1954, trick roper and TV cowboy Montie Montana rode into the Commerce Trust lobby. His horse, Rex, feigned eating cash out of money bags from the Commerce vault as, at far left, James Kemper, Sr. looks on (no money was eaten). Right, a customer's passbook showed withdrawals and deposits neatly recorded for every transaction.

The kidnapping of Bobby Greenlease, the six-year-old son of a prominent Kansas City auto dealer, in 1953 led to the largest ransom payout in U.S. history at the time. Quick thinking by Commerce Trust helped authorities find the kidnappers, above. The bank used cameras from its transit department to photograph the ransom money. With the serial numbers recorded by Commerce, authorities tracked the money to St. Louis. They located the kidnappers and took them into custody—the crime was solved quickly, thanks to the help of the employees at Commerce Trust.

customers of the period went on to become multi-billion-dollar enterprises, including H&R Block, Trans World Airlines and Marion Laboratories.

Brothers Henry and Richard Bloch started tax preparation service H&R Block (initially called United Business Company) in Kansas City in 1946 with the help of a $5,000 loan from Commerce. Their father, Leon Bloch, was a prominent Kansas City lawyer who had opened the family's first account with Commerce nearly three decades earlier. Henry Bloch gave Commerce's Harry Wuerth, Arthur Eisenhower's successor as chief lending officer, the credit for H&R Block's growth into what would become

the world's largest tax service, noting in 1970 that "we never would have grown from a one-room bookkeeping operation to an international business with nearly 4,400 offices without Harry's creative financial guidance."

Henry Bloch would often tell the story of how Commerce carefully tracked his account. When he was in World War II, he wasn't writing checks, and the bank declined the first check he wrote after returning home because his signature didn't match the one on his account when he opened it. "It probably had changed," said Bloch. "I admired them for it. At least they were paying attention."

Loans from Commerce helped Kansas City grow and

LIFETIME PASS

GOOD FOR UNLIMITED USAGE ON THE

Commerce Trust Company

GLIDING ELECTRIC STAIRS

This pass is our good guarantee
That you can ESCALATE for free.
May your ups-and-downs be smooth and neat,
And restful on your legs and feet!

In the fall of 1955, Commerce installed new "electric stairs" in the Walnut Lobby of its headquarters building, with James Kemper, Sr. and Arthur Eisenhower leading the way on the maiden voyage. The bank gave Lifetime Passes to those who rode the escalator on opening day. Opposite, Commerce opened its first "motor bank" in December 1957; it featured hand-operated drawers, a pneumatic tube to exchange money and documents, and closed-circuit television monitoring for security.

Civic Involvement

James Kemper, Sr. spent much of his career with Commerce Bank developing and nurturing an interest in the economic vitality of the Kansas City region.

By 1940, downtown Kansas City suffered from post-Depression neglect, with buildings closed and parking nearly non-existent. Kemper became chairman of the Downtown Committee, later known as the Downtown Redevelopment Corporation, that year—and by the end of the year, Commerce had purchased land at Tenth and Main next to its headquarters and built a parking garage that eventually housed the first Commerce Motorbank. It opened to the public in June 1941, helping to alleviate the city's parking problem.

In December 1943, Kemper joined with other civic leaders to establish the nonprofit Midwest Research Institute (MRI) to conduct research and offer consulting services in agriculture, mining, transportation and manufacturing in the Midwest. MRI opened in June 1944, and one of its first jobs was to help convert ammonium nitrate plants in Kansas and Arkansas from World War II munitions factories into fertilizer plants. In the 1950s, the institute developed the technology used by the Mars candy company to coat 3,300 pounds of chocolate an hour for M&M's candies, and it developed the first process of freeze-drying coffee for the Kansas City–based Folger Coffee Company.

Kemper continued his work redeveloping Kansas City's downtown in the late 1940s. He advocated for new expressways to ease downtown traffic, and in the 1950s, pushed for a beautification effort around then-derelict Union Station Plaza (now Hallmark's Crown Center), noting, "Kansas City is a beautiful city, and we should eliminate these eyesores." Kemper also commissioned the *Muse of Missouri* sculpture and fountain—placed in memory of his late son David—in a prominent traffic island on Main Street between Eighth and Ninth streets. It was dedicated in 1963.

Downtown improvement remained Kemper's major effort later in life. In 1953, he had a 3,300-pound clock costing $16,000 installed outside the bank, and it became a landmark for visitors to Kansas City. In 1956, his Downtown Improvement Corporation constructed 811 Main Street as an operations headquarters for the Long Lines Division of AT&T, then based in Kansas City. (This 250,000-square-foot building now houses Commerce's operations and bank card groups.) On its north façade, he installed a pair of 10-foot bronze bas-relief sculptures of jazz players, honoring Kansas City's jazz tradition. One of the musicians has the number "8-1/2" inscribed on the sole of his shoe—not his shoe size, but rather the Eighth Street address of a speakeasy once located nearby.

In 1960, the bank announced plans to build the Commerce Tower office building on Main Street. When it opened in 1965, the Commerce Tower was the tallest commercial building in Missouri, with 30 stories and 488,000 square feet of office space. For its sunken

Commerce has a long tradition of working to promote and keep downtown Kansas City a vibrant center of the region. During his leadership, James Kemper, Sr. considered this work essential to a healthy business. Kemper dedicated the Muse of Missouri *sculpture, left, as a memorial to his son, David Woods Kemper, killed in Italy during the last days of World War II. Commerce Tower, opposite, seen under construction in August 1963, led to a renaissance in business and culture in downtown Kansas City. The William T. Kemper Foundation, formed in 1989 with the generous bequest of William T. Kemper, Jr., opposite, has become one of the Kemper family's key vehicles for leadership and support of culture, education and civic improvement.*

garden off Main Street, James Kemper, Jr. commissioned a large bronze avant-garde fountain by the Seattle artist George Tsutakawa. In the adjacent space, the Myron Green Cafeteria organization operated a casual restaurant and bar named Magnolia II, appropriately recalling the Magnolia Saloon over which Francis Long first operated his bank in 1865.

James Kemper, Jr. carried on his father's tradition of community service, becoming a member of the University of Kansas City (now University of Missouri-Kansas City) board in the 1950s and a member of the Kansas City Public School Board in the early 1960s. He also spearheaded development of Oppenstein Brothers Memorial Park in downtown Kansas City and in 1981 founded the Downtown Council, a civic group whose mission is to foster a vibrant and economically sustainable business district in the city's center. Kemper was the council's first president. It now has 300 members. In 1989, the William T. Kemper Foundation was established and is dedicated to William T. Kemper, Jr.'s lifelong interest in improving the human condition and quality of life. It focuses its giving on education, health and human services, the arts and civic improvements.

He Meant Business

Ewing Kauffman was a 35-year-old pharmaceutical super-salesman who had just started a calcium supplements business in his basement when, in 1951, he asked Commerce Bank for a $5,000 loan to expand. He earned $900 in profit in his first year, selling a medicinal tablet called OS-Cal made from crushed oyster shells— making sales calls and producing and packaging his product by day, then processing orders and typing labels at night.

Recognizing an entrepreneur who would succeed, Commerce loaned Kauffman the money and continued to back him for decades as his Kansas City–based business, Marion Laboratories, grew and became a major national pharmaceutical firm. Establishing a niche in the industry by acquiring companies that had discovered drugs but not brought them to market, Marion Labs reached $1 billion in revenue and had the highest sales and profit per employee of any corporation on the New York Stock Exchange in 1989. Dow Chemical purchased a controlling interest in Marion that year, eventually combining it with its Merrell Dow pharmaceutical division into Marion Merrell Dow, now part of French pharmaceutical giant Sanofi.

Commerce did more than help Kauffman build his company. It helped him buy a Major League Baseball team, the Kansas City Royals, in 1969. As Kauffman recalled in a 1971 interview with the *Kansas City Star*, to negotiate the purchase, "I went to Chicago where the American League meeting took place. Commerce Bank was good enough to give me a $6 million letter of credit as evidence that I meant business."

Today, the Royals are owned by David Glass, chief executive officer of Wal-Mart Stores Inc., who purchased the team in 2000 after seven years of running it on behalf of the Kansas City Community Foundation following Kauffman's death. Commerce is still the Royals' bank, making seasonal loans and providing credit card services both to the team and to devoted fans.

Of Commerce, Glass said, "They've handled all of our financial needs. Anything we have asked them to do, they have done. They have also been great supporters, sponsors and advertisers."

Ewing Kauffman, the founding owner of the Kansas City Royals, established the team with a line of credit from Commerce; Commerce has supported the baseball team's financial needs ever since. Above, the check Kauffman wrote to pay the Royals' American League membership fee in 1968 was issued by Commerce Bank.

become better connected to the world at a time when fast, efficient travel was becoming essential to American society and business. Trans World Airlines, founded in Kansas City in the 1930s, had a terminal at the city's old municipal airport and a service facility at the former B-25 Mitchell bomber base at Fairfax Airport in Kansas City, Kansas. In 1947, James Kemper, Sr. and Arthur Eisenhower helped the airline underwrite a bond offering to build a new overhaul base on land north of the city that had been earmarked for a future international airport; an Eastern bank had declined to underwrite the offering. After carefully analyzing TWA's financial statements, James Sr. determined that the bond

After New York banks declined to finance a new Trans World Airlines' operations center, Commerce Trust stepped up to underwrite the project's bonds. The TWA Overhaul Base, 18 miles north of downtown, at its peak provided more than 5,000 jobs and led to the opening of Kansas City International airport in 1972.

offering would be a safe investment, and, with the bank's support, the new overhaul facility was built in the mid-1950s. It was a centerpiece of the city's new Mid-Continent International Airport, whose first runway opened in 1956. By 1972, TWA had become Kansas City's largest employer, with some 6,000 employees, and Mid-Continent Airport had been rebuilt and renamed Kansas City International Airport.

John Brown, who would succeed Harry Wuerth as chief credit officer in 1970, recalled the story of a small but growing telephone company in Abilene, Kansas, called United Utilities as an example of the careful study Commerce gave to loan requests: After United made multiple presentations to the loan committee, Commerce committed to provide the company the maximum credit line allowed any customer at the time. United used this credit to expand into new markets. Five years later, its success prompted a name change to United Telecommunications, and by the mid-1970s, it was a $1 billion company servicing 3.5 million local telephone lines in cities from coast to coast. That company is now Sprint, which in 2014 was the third largest wireless telecommunications operator in the United States.

Commerce's strategy in commercial lending was to partner with promising companies early in their development and nurture them to maturity. As Wuerth explained, "One of the greatest thrills in banking is to take a small business with modest means and eager, intelligent management, and be a part of its growth. Any banker can handle a loan to an established major corporation. The real challenge—and reward—is to place your faith in a small, struggling business and help it move forward."

As the 1950s progressed, James Kemper, Jr. took on greater responsibility at the bank. In 1955, he was elected president at the age of 34. His earlier war service and professional experience would help him lead Commerce through a series of changes that put the bank on the front lines of banking consolidation well into the 1970s.

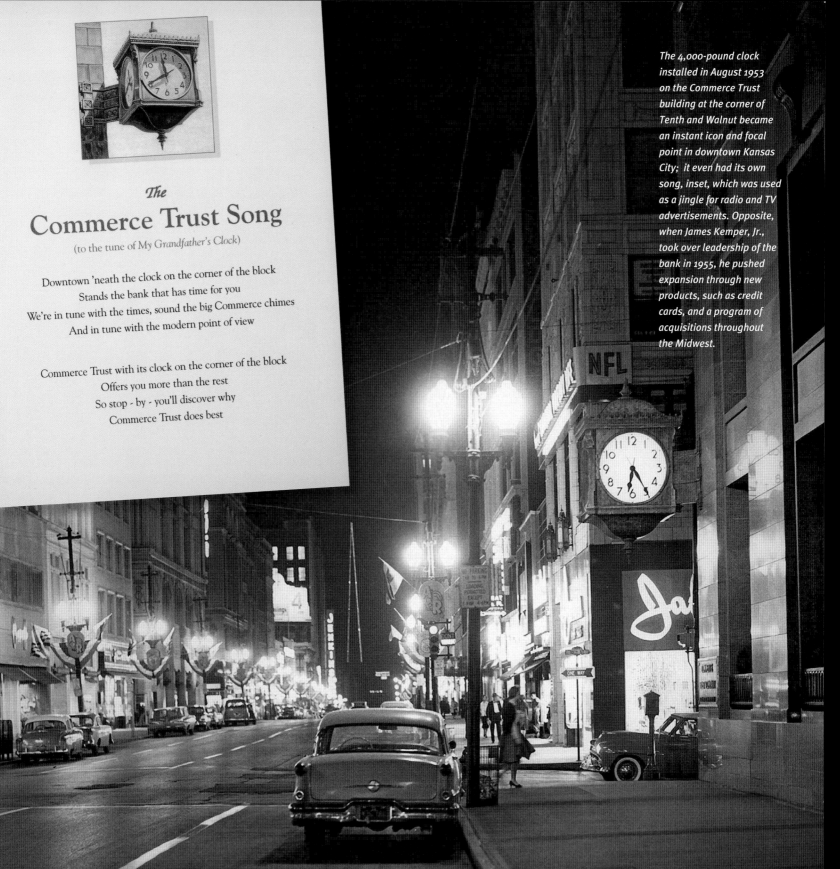

The
Commerce Trust Song

(to the tune of *My Grandfather's Clock*)

Downtown 'neath the clock on the corner of the block
Stands the bank that has time for you
We're in tune with the times, sound the big Commerce chimes
And in tune with the modern point of view

Commerce Trust with its clock on the corner of the block
Offers you more than the rest
So stop - by - you'll discover why
Commerce Trust does best

The 4,000-pound clock installed in August 1953 on the Commerce Trust building at the corner of Tenth and Walnut became an instant icon and focal point in downtown Kansas City; it even had its own song, inset, which was used as a jingle for radio and TV advertisements. Opposite, when James Kemper, Jr., took over leadership of the bank in 1955, he pushed expansion through new products, such as credit cards, and a program of acquisitions throughout the Midwest.

Members of the Kansas City Chiefs football team signed the beam during the topping-out ceremony for Commerce Tower, a Kansas City landmark. From left, the players are Chris Burford, E.J. Holub, Jerry Mays, Len Dawson and Abner Haynes (the boy's identity is unknown). Commerce sold the tower in 2006. Opposite, Commerce produced a household-hints booklet in the 1960s to help customers save time and money.

THE SUPER COMMUNITY BANK

James Kemper, Sr. ran Commerce Trust in a way that reflected the world of the late 1940s and 1950s, a time of economic growth and prosperity across the United States. Commerce stuck to its knitting, attended to its core business, established a toehold in some new areas, and saw its profits increase as it made loans to growing households and expanding enterprises.

However, with new times came new opportunities and challenges. James Kemper, Jr. had a strong personal vision about the direction of banking, and, as he gained responsibility for day-to-day operations in the mid-1950s, he looked for ways to grow the bank that his father had not considered. Banks in other parts of the country were opening branches and buying smaller banks, and James Jr. wanted to do the same. When he became chairman of Commerce Trust in November 1964, he had everything he needed: he was fully in control of a very strong bank, and changes to state and federal banking laws would enable it to grow in new ways.

COMMERCE TOWER
COMMERCE TRUST COMPANY

A couple leaves the new Commerce Tower in a picture taken shortly after the building's 1965 completion.

BUILDING THE STATEWIDE NETWORK

Congress had passed the Bank Holding Company Act in 1956, allowing banks to set up holding companies that could acquire other banks in states where they were headquartered. Missouri marginally loosened its branch banking laws three years later, allowing banks to have drive-through locations separate from their main offices—as long as these were within 1,000 yards of the main location and at least 400 feet away from a competitor.

In August 1966, Commerce formed a holding company named Commerce Bancshares, Inc., to acquire other banks throughout Missouri and build a statewide network of affiliated offices. With the Federal Reserve's approval, the holding company acquired the stock of Commerce Trust in early 1967. "The holding company, in our view, is the best way to grow in a non-branching situation," said Kemper.

Moving at a deliberate pace, he first acquired Merriman Mortgage, a Kansas City-based residential mortgage company. By November 1967, Commerce had signed preliminary agreements to acquire three Missouri banks that had previously been valued correspondent customers: Citizens Bank of Joplin, Charlton County Exchange Bank in Brunswick and The Citizens Bank of Springfield. Kemper and his team were very familiar with their operations as well as with their management, and they were confident of their potential to build Commerce in new communities. Among the reasons for their optimism were that Commerce deliberately acquired banks that were culturally similar and that, as a general rule, it retained the management, staff and customers of the acquired banks.

"We were making deals in banks interested in selling to us, and with people not resting on their laurels," Kemper said. "The main problem was gaining the confidence of the banks that there was more money in selling the bank than running it. If you got to talking to someone and they liked you, they would listen to you." He explained his acquisition philosophy in 1968:

First of all, there must be a desire on the part of the bank's present management and stockholders to ally themselves with our group. Second, there must be a mutually agreed upon management concept based on sound, aggressive banking, with proper return to stockholders and opportunity for adequate remuneration and advancement for management. Third, we consider the attitude of the bank's community

This Kansas City Star *article from March 21, 1965, noted that the new Commerce Tower would have* "a population of 3,500 ... its own post office, its own transportation system (vertical, not horizontal), its own restaurants, barber shop, park and art gallery [and] a power plant bigger than many cities have."

A Soaring New Tower On the City's Skyline

By Fred Fitzsimmons
(The Star's Real Estate Editor)

IT will be a "city" with a daytime population of 3,500.

That's bigger than 82 per cent of the nearly 1,000 cities of Missouri and Kansas, or about the size of Scott City, Kas., or Harrisonville, Mo.

To extend the analogy, it has its own postoffice, its own transportation system (vertical, not horizontal), its own restaurants, barber shop, park and art gallery, a power plant bigger than many cities have.

It provides 12 acres more or less for commerce, entertainment, instruction and service.

In two words, it is the Commerce Tower.

Public Opening Today

The 32-story skyscraper (plus two sublevels) at Ninth and Main streets has had some tenants since early this year. For the last six weeks, its distinctive Top of the Tower restaurant complex has been functioning. Similarly, many groups and individuals have inspected the dining area and, to a lesser degree, parts of the overall building.

Today and tomorrow, the Commerce Tower opens its doors to the general public. Tens of thousands of persons are expected, says the Commerce Trust company, sponsor of the 12-million-dollar structure. Both days, the building will be on display from 9 to 5 o'clock.

Then, on Friday, April 2, the formal dedication will take place, on the broad plaza area on the Main street side.

Commerce Trust officials say the 542,800-square-foot building, largest private office structure in Missouri, is 80 per cent leased. Commitments are on hand for another 10 per cent of the space. This is an exceedingly high rate of acceptance for a building of this size and character. Often it takes many months for a large office building, created speculatively, to become fully leased.

A Long Walk Indoors

To date, nearly 80 firms have acquired space in the Commerce Tower, including the Commerce Trust company. The bank facilities will be in all or part of the first through fifth floors, even though the commercial banking functions will remain in the present Tenth and Walnut streets building, to

which the Tower is physically attached.

(An intriguing aspect of this attachment: It soon will be possible to walk from the Tenth and Walnut lobby to the lobby of the Prom Sheraton motor-hotel at Sixth and Main — indoors. There is a covered passageway over Ninth street linking the Tower with the 811 Main building and garage, which in turn will have an underpass below Eighth street connecting with the expanded Prom between Seventh and Eighth streets. The Prom expansion and the older part of the motel will be joined both

below and above Seventh street.)

In addition to the bank space, major Tower occupants will be, or are, the Aetna Casualty & Surety company and Aetna Life Insurance company; Gustin-Bacon Manufacturing company, the Mayfair-Lennox Hotels (operator of the Top of the Tower restaurants), Fireman's Fund Insurance company and Arthur Andersen & Co., all with square footage occupancies in five figures.

Tenants range downward to a 100-square-foot office tenancy of the Acme Reporting service.

(Continued on Page 19.)

Water, light and bronze form an animate sculpture as a focal point in the Commerce Tower's sunken garden. The 13-foot high free-form figure and fountain are the design of George Tsutakawa, West Coast artist. On two sides of the garden is the Garden gallery, devoted to the exhibition of art works and, later, a casual luncheon area.

Commerce Tower Section

THE KANSAS CITY STAR

Sunday, March 21, 1965

● Woman's Touch in Design. 2D   ● Banking in Two Buildings 15D
● Dining in the Clouds...... 6D   ● Evolution of a Skyscraper. 16D

SECTION D

Rising 30 stories above Kansas City and totaling 438,000 square feet, Commerce Tower was at the time of its construction the largest commercial building in Missouri—a fitting landmark for a company feeling a larger sense of its role and potential in the Midwest. For Commerce as well as for the city of Kansas City, the tower marked the start of a revitalization of downtown. The building's 30th floor housed The Top of the Tower with themed restaurants serving Mongolian, Italian, Austrian and French food. There was also an Irish pub with a thatched roof, a futuristic Control Tower lounge and a banquet room known as the Tower Suite. Visitors and people who had moved to the suburbs enjoyed fine dining in a unique setting with stunning views of Kansas City.

James Kemper, Jr.'s strategy in the late 1960s and 1970s grew Commerce by acquiring banks throughout Missouri. Kemper and his executive team paused during a visit to Springfield, Missouri, where Commerce acquired Citizens Bank in 1967. Left to right, the men are P. V. "Plez" Miller, Jr., president of Commerce Trust; John Leffen, president of Commerce's bank in Joplin; Kemper; Walter Riffle, chairman of Commerce's Brunswick bank; Thomas Watkins, chairman of the Springfield bank; and James Jeffries, who was president of Citizens Bank before Commerce purchased it. Right, a 1970s-era pin studded with a diamond and two sapphires marked 25 years of service with Commerce Bank.

toward the growth of that community and its desire for an alliance with other communities throughout the state to build sound businesses and worthy social and cultural institutions under good government.

As Commerce acquired new affiliates, it adopted a highly decentralized model, giving local managers of the acquired banks relatively great autonomy as long as they operated prudently within Commerce's rules and business philosophy. Acquired banks maintained their local boards of directors, and when needed, they could depend on Commerce's holding company staff for assistance with services such as advertising, auditing and data processing. As Kemper explained:

While, of course, each of our member banks must maintain its own autonomy and identity and be ultimately responsible for its own decisions, we must always keep an open mind as to what can be accomplished by our joint efforts to launch new services. I think we will find that often the fastest learners and the most imaginative producers in our group will come from the relatively smaller members of our holding company family. In short, each affiliate bank may count on the full support of the parent organization, but will not be subjected to domination by it.

Executive Vice President Bill Lamberson, at right, with Kemper, was one of James Kemper, Jr.'s key executives in the 1960s. Others included Plez Miller, president of Commerce Trust, and Harry Wuerth, chief credit officer. Opposite, Commerce entered the credit card business in 1968, becoming one of the first non–New York banks to do so. Three models pose with an enlarged BankAmericard in front of a photo of Commerce Tower, and the inset shows an early Commerce ad for its MasterCard, both from the late 1960s.

The acquisition of Springfield's Citizens Bank took place according to this playbook. As John Himmel, who would later lead the Springfield bank as regional chairman and CEO, said, "What made the Springfield market so successful is that we continued to build on the success of what we acquired."

Community by community, Commerce expanded its footprint. By early 1969, Commerce made offers to purchase banks in Kirksville, St. Joseph, St. Charles, University City and Kirkwood. Commerce's reputation for strength and character helped make this easier. The CEO of the bank in St. Joseph, for example, approached Kemper and said, "I've decided I want to merge with your bank because you're

the best bank, and here's my price." By the end of the year, Commerce had also offered to buy banks in Columbia, Tipton, Mexico and Hannibal.

Kemper, speaking to residents of Mexico, Missouri, in 1970, said, "We are building our concept of the Commerce family of banking on community service, and we wish to be judged in our new concept of Missouri banking on this issue. We feel that we can operate soundly and solvently and render increasing customer service."

Under James Kemper, Jr.'s leadership, Commerce was now one of the fastest-growing banks in the country—while continuing to honor its community roots. "Some banks may be like anteaters, and some may seem more like elephants," Kemper said at the time. "But you can't ever be much more than what you are. And a banker shouldn't try to move in where he's not an expert."

At the end of 1970, James Kemper changed the Kansas City bank's name from Commerce Trust Company to Commerce Bank of Kansas City, adopting the Commerce Bank trade style for all of its affiliated banks. As the new decade began, the holding company neared $1 billion in assets.

CHARGE IT, PLEASE

Diners Club introduced the first credit card in the United States in 1950, but it wasn't until the 1960s that credit cards gained widespread use. Bank of America launched the BankAmericard program in California in 1958, and in 1965 it started licensing the card to banks outside its home state. Bank of America approached Commerce to see if it wanted a credit card territory in the Midwest. Commerce said yes, and in April 1968 it became the first bank in the credit card business in Missouri; it also issued cards in Kansas and Nebraska, although it later sold the Nebraska business to concentrate on Missouri and Kansas.

The initial results were not promising. According to Warren Weaver, who joined the bank in 1968 and later became head of the credit card business, Commerce had to convince retailers to accept the card. Furthermore, the bank initially experienced substantial losses in credit cards. Commerce stayed with the business, though, recognizing that consumer credit was the way of the future. As the bank learned how credit cards worked and saw how customers used them, it developed a better process for identifying the risks. Commerce realized that a consumer's creditworthiness could be evaluated based on his or her credit history, and soon the bank was applying the same rigorous approach to risk evaluation in accepting credit card customers

Starting in the 1920s with
Ford's Model T and spurred
by the construction of the
interstate highway system
in the 1950s, the nation's
car culture created strong
demand for new and used
cars—and the loans
consumers needed to
purchase them. Commerce
used billboards such as this
to promote its auto loans.

that it used in making business and personal loans.

"Credit cards are a risky business because of the potential for credit and fraud losses," Weaver said. "Unlike most bank lending, card lending is unsecured, but when the business is operated prudently, customers benefit greatly and the business can be profitable."

Commerce operated its card business well—so well, in fact, that as other banks struggled with and sold their card businesses under duress in the late 1970s and '80s, Commerce successfully expanded its credit card operation—continuing to provide customers with credit and giving the bank a diversified stream of revenue and profits. Commerce had particular success with an idea championed by James Kemper, Jr.: the combined credit and ATM card, introduced in 1984 under the name Special Connections. The first such bank card product, it brought together two previously

separate operations of the bank—deposits and credit—and gave customers a single, easy way to pay for purchases, using either credit or available cash. In addition to providing a new customer benefit, Special Connections deepened Commerce's relationship with its customers and gave the bank a competitive advantage over other banks.

Credit cards were just one of several areas into which the bank expanded during Kemper's first two decades as Commerce's leader. By the end of the 1970s, the bank also created a subsidiary to help other banks with document and data processing, and another that was a reinsurer for credit life insurance and accident and health insurance. Commerce also began an ambitious program of placing cash dispensing machines—and later ATMs, automated teller machines—outside its branches so customers could get cash, make deposits or transfer funds after banking hours.

Supporting a Passion

With Commerce Bank's help, Johnny Morris turned his love of bass fishing into one of the country's most successful retailers of outdoor gear. As a 24-year-old budding entrepreneur, Morris was determined to make a career out of one of his greatest passions, and he was disappointed but undeterred when the department store near his home wouldn't stock the lures and other gear he needed to become a competitive fisherman.

In 1971, he rented a U-Haul trailer and drove around the country, stocking up on professional-quality equipment. He convinced his father, who had founded the Brown Derby liquor store chain in Springfield, Missouri, to set aside a small area at the back of one of the stores, and there he opened a bait and tackle shop. It was ideally situated on the main road to the tourist destinations of Branson and Table Rock Lake, and Morris was successful from the start. With a year of business under his belt, on his father's suggestion he approached Commerce to ask for a business loan. He obtained a line of credit, with which he opened a second store and, in 1974, began publishing a direct-mail catalog.

Some 40 years later, Morris is majority owner of a $4 billion enterprise that includes 90 Bass Pro Shops stores in North America, a manufacturer of fishing boats and a resort in the Missouri Ozarks. In addition to providing Morris with his first credit line and continuing to loan his company money for four decades, Commerce helped line up a consortium of other lenders. The bank also designed, installed and operates Bass Pro Shops' credit card processing system and is a proud contributor to Bass Pro's golf tournament to raise funds for college scholarships.

"At every stage of development of the company, Commerce has been right there," said Morris, and he meant that literally: he and John Himmel, the former chairman of Commerce Bank's Springfield Region,

fished together often, deepening their friendship as well as Himmel's understanding of his customer's business. "As our company has grown and we have reached out more broadly to a group of banks to support us, Commerce, besides being one of those lenders, has been very steadfast with their guidance," Morris said. "We view Commerce as our family. They took the time to care and to get involved. They understand us."

Johnny Morris, left, president of Bass Pro Shops and Tracker Marine, shows Kenneth Carter, then-president of Commerce Bank of Springfield, a fishing reel at the Bass Pro Shops' Outdoor World showroom in Springfield in 1989.

Commerce held an open house after it acquired Manchester Financial and gained its first major presence in St. Louis in 1978. From left: George Guernsey, III, president of Commerce Bank of St. Louis; John M. Murphy, CPA; Angela Mazzola, customer service officer with Commerce-Manchester Bank; J. Charles Clardy, secretary-treasurer of the Metropolitan St. Louis Sewer District; and Albert F. Toczylowski, controller of INTRAV Inc.

A NEW GENERATION

At the same time James Kemper, Jr. was growing the bank, he was also preparing the next generation of leaders to carry on the traditions that he and his predecessors had worked hard to instill at Commerce. He had four children—two sons and two daughters—and three of them played significant roles in the bank's operations beginning in the 1970s. Laura Kemper, the oldest, worked for nearly a decade as vice president of marketing and oversaw creation of the bank's first television commercials. Sons David and Jonathan grew up seeing their father work at the bank, and both spent time as teenagers working there themselves.

David, the older son, graduated from Harvard and received a master's degree in English literature from Oxford before earning an MBA from Stanford in 1976. Out of college, he took a job in commercial lending with JP Morgan. During one visit home, he told his father that the

Upgrading its computer systems in the 1960s and '70s was critical to Commerce as it used new digital technology to support its expanding business. State-of-the art data storage devices—tape drives—were located in the bank's data processing center in the Commerce Tower around 1970. Commerce's advertising, including the brochure and button promoting the bank's checking accounts, below, reflected the psychedelic look of the early 1970s.

zip
application

THE BIG CASH CUSHION CHECKING PLUS

THE BIG CASH CUSHION CHECKING PLUS

IBM 7330
MAGNETIC TAPE UNIT

Commerce Trust's remarkable new checking service that puts a big cash cushion in your checkbook... lets you write checks bigger than your balance.

bank intended to move him overseas. His father asked David to consider a job with Commerce instead, and in 1978, David joined the bank in commercial lending. "I enjoyed it," David said. "It was the heart and soul of the business." After three years, David was assigned to strategic planning.

Kemper's younger son, Jonathan, entered the banking industry after graduating from Harvard with an undergraduate degree in 1975 and an MBA in 1979. He worked for the Federal Reserve in New York and held various positions at financial services companies in New York and Chicago, including Citicorp and M. A. Schapiro and Company. His father approached him in 1982 and said, "This would be a good time to come back. We'd like to know your plans." Jonathan joined Commerce that year as a vice president and loan officer, managing large commercial relationships.

IT TAKES A TEAM

It was no coincidence that David and Jonathan held respected positions with other companies before returning to Missouri to begin their Commerce careers. It was important to James Kemper, Jr. that his children work elsewhere after graduation—that they gain knowledge, experience and perspective in the outside world, and that any choice they might make to enter the family business be conscious and well informed. He wanted them to join

the bank with confidence, the ability to handle significant responsibility and the likelihood that they'd be taken seriously by other employees.

James Kemper, Jr. laid thoughtful groundwork for the entrance of his sons into the family business. As Jonathan recalled, he "really assembled a tremendous team anticipating our return. He made a special point of giving us responsibility at the bank and opportunities to perform."

The management team James Jr. had assembled was indeed a strong group. Among the many leaders and innovators he hired or promoted were Warren Weaver, who would become president of Commerce Bank of Kansas City in 1982; Bob Matthews, who joined the bank in 1969 as a credit analyst and would become chief credit officer in 1989; A. Bayard Clark, who would become chief financial

officer in the 1990s after overseeing mergers and acquisitions in the 1980s; John Himmel, who was hired in 1973 and would become chairman and CEO of Commerce's bank in Springfield; and Charles Kim, a young talent when he was hired in 1982 who would rise to become executive vice president and chief financial officer.

Weaver said employees welcomed the hiring of Kemper's sons because of the Kemper family's success in running the bank. "All of them are smart, and all of them work hard," Weaver said. "In a short time, you realized this made sense." That's a good thing, because as Commerce moved into the 1980s and the industry around it began to rapidly consolidate, the bank would need all the intelligence, innovation and perspective it could muster if it were to remain a leader in its markets.

The company's board of directors in 1979 comprised, front row, from left: John A. Morgan, P.V. Miller, Jr., Menefee "Chuck" Blackwell, James Kemper, Jr., Robert M. White, II, Thomas B. Donahue and James E. McClure. Back row, from left: Edward T. McNally, Bill Lamberson, Morton Sosland, Charles M. Ruprecht, Joseph H. McGee, Jr., Paul Mueller, George H. Pfister and William E. Leffen.

Commerce achieved statewide scope in Missouri in the early 1980s, setting the stage for even greater expansion to come. By 1983, it had achieved the critical mass it wanted in the St. Louis market and, as shown on a location map, opposite, published by the bank that year, had similarly solid footing in other communities in the eastern and western sides of the state.

GATEWAY TO GROWTH

It's sometimes said that St. Louis is the country's westernmost Eastern city and Kansas City the easternmost Western city—the communities' cultures very different and their eyes turned in opposite directions for inspiration and trends in business, fashion, entertainment and other matters. True as that may be, Commerce Bank ultimately found a way to bridge the divide and is now considered the hometown bank in both cities.

As early as mid-1971, James Kemper, Jr. had been studying the possibility of opening a bank in St. Louis. To that date, no Kansas City bank had been able to enter the St. Louis market with impact. Commerce had acquired three small banks in the suburbs in the late 1960s, but none were in St. Louis itself.

Many people noted the challenge a bank from the other side of the state would have putting a stake solidly in the ground in St. Louis, but Kemper saw things more dispassionately and pragmatically: "St. Louis is the biggest banking market in the state, and we feel we should be represented in it," he said.

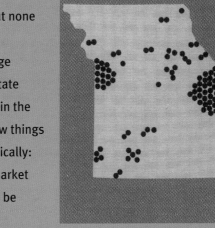

When Commerce completed its acquisition of County Tower Bank in 1983, it moved into County Tower's headquarters building in the St. Louis suburb of Clayton and used that location as the base from which to build its business in the metro area. Because Commerce has headquarters staff in both Kansas City and St. Louis, the former County Tower building—situated in what is now Commerce's largest metropolitan market—houses the offices of many of Commerce's top executives.

Commerce Bank

ACQUIRING COUNTY TOWER

Indeed, St. Louis was a critical market for Commerce. In 1970, the St. Louis region had approximately 2.5 million residents; Kansas City was about half its size, at 1.4 million. To gain scale and be recognized as a truly statewide bank, it needed a presence in the state's largest metro area. Quoted at the time in the industry publication *American Banker*, Kemper remarked that St. Louis would benefit from some "fresh points of view in banking to tackle areas where the city has lagged."

In November 1972, the Federal Reserve approved Commerce's application to open a new bank in St. Louis— over the objection of competitor banks that thought the move would violate state branch banking laws intended to prevent banking concentration. The Fed accepted Commerce's argument that the new bank would not eliminate competitors and that the four banks Commerce already controlled in the area held less than 2 percent of the region's deposits. Commerce Bank of St. Louis opened on December 15, 1972, achieving Kemper's goal of establishing a presence on both sides of Missouri.

With a foothold in St. Louis, Kemper began scouting the area for other acquisition partners. In 1974, Commerce acquired the Valley Bank of Florissant in a suburb northwest of St. Louis. Four years later, it purchased St. Louis-based Manchester Financial, which owned Manchester Bank, a three-bank holding company with a total of $163 million in deposits. By the end of 1978, Commerce had nine banks in the area with $414 million in deposits: a 4.8 percent market share.

The Manchester Financial acquisition made Commerce the fourth largest bank in the St. Louis market, but size didn't equal

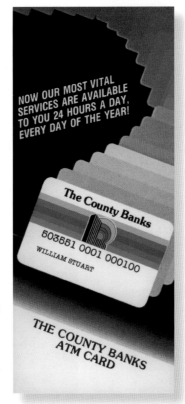

success, and building a major presence in St. Louis remained a critically important goal.

For five years, Commerce pressed for success in St. Louis—promoting its name, its services and its brand values, acquiring smaller area banks, building its business and generally becoming more involved with the community. By the first quarter of 1983, Commerce had 14 banks in the St. Louis area, with total assets of $679 million and loans of $363 million on the books—good, but not the critical mass Commerce was seeking.

Finally, in 1983, Kemper identified an opportunity to substantially strengthen the bank's foothold in St. Louis. The key was County Tower Corporation, a $1 billion bank based in Clayton, a major St. Louis suburb, with nine locations in total. As the largest independent bank in St. Louis County, County Tower made an ideal partner, with a good reputation and excellent standing in the business community. Commerce executives approached their counterparts at County Tower to discuss a possible merger, but the talks went nowhere.

In June 1983, James Kemper was approached by a major County Tower shareholder who had tried to sell his 8.4 percent share of the bank's stock back to County Tower and was not satisfied with the price being offered. After Kemper checked with County Tower executives who had declined to purchase these holdings, Commerce acquired them itself. While Commerce and County Tower executives held several meetings after Commerce acquired the shares, County Tower filed a lawsuit attempting to pre-empt any acquisition attempt. Kemper did not intend to acquire the bank in a hostile manner, and, instead negotiated an agreement to buy the rest of County Tower at an increased price. The $99 million,

The acquisition of County Tower Bank more than doubled Commerce's St. Louis-area market share and made Commerce the largest bank statewide in terms of branches, with 111. The merger also gave Commerce deeper connections with St. Louis business leaders. County Bank's ATM card in the early 1980s, left, gave customers access to their accounts and the ability to deposit and withdraw money 24 hours a day.

John Capps, a St. Louis businessman and long-term Commerce customer, operated a network of auto dealerships and currently oversees family investments, including major real estate holdings. Now a member of Commerce Bank's board of directors, Capps chose Commerce because of its long-term perspective and community orientation: "You want to do business with somebody you respect and admire," he says. In 1984, Commerce rolled out Special Connections, right, the first card in the market to combine the features of a credit card and an ATM card.

all-cash transaction was announced in August and closed in January 1984.

With the County Tower acquisition, Commerce now had the most banking offices in Missouri, 107, and was the state's third largest bank in deposits, assets and loans. The transaction more than doubled Commerce's share of the St. Louis market.

THERE FOR THE LONG HAUL

While the County Tower acquisition would prove hugely beneficial in the long run, the bank's management initially presented a challenge for Commerce. Having voted themselves generous "golden parachutes" that were triggered by the acquisition, several County Tower senior executives left immediately after the deal closed—presenting a challenge to a bank trying to maintain continuity in a new market. Continuity is important to any business, and it is

especially so in banking, where business is often based on personal relationships and trust.

Kemper realized that to succeed in St. Louis, he needed to immediately have a strong leadership team in place. The bank engaged an executive search firm to find new managers to run the acquired bank, but none satisfied Kemper, so he asked his son David to make the move to St. Louis to manage the bank's growing operations there. Commerce executive Warren Weaver, who would soon become the bank's president, recalled a meeting he attended with the Kempers in which father told son, "Either you or I have to go to St. Louis, and I'm not moving."

David Kemper moved with his family to St. Louis in 1985, excited at the prospect of constructing something sustainable there, ready to cultivate relationships in the community and eager to settle in for the long term. Reflecting later on the County Tower episode, David remarked "It was the best deal we have made for a bank. It was a huge opportunity."

David's strategy was to build the St. Louis business "one customer at a time," according to Bayard Clark, who joined Commerce in the Manchester Financial acquisition and, as an executive vice president of Commerce-Manchester, provided input on potential St. Louis–area acquisitions. David met regularly with directors and other local businessmen to learn from them about the city. "David made it a habit to have lunch with someone in a leadership role in St. Louis every day of the week," Clark said. "Usually something would come up at the lunch where the bank could help."

David began joining a number of well-respected

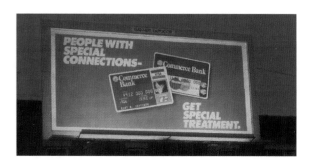

community organizations and, by 1988, he had become the youngest member of Civic Progress, a group of St. Louis' most influential leaders. He was a member of several boards, including that of Washington University, where he is a past chairman, and the Missouri Botanical Garden, where he is a past president. "If we're going to have a big operation," David Kemper said at the time, "we've got to show a commitment."

Commerce's efforts to develop roots in St. Louis has had a great return—initially in the bank's short-term image and performance in the community and, longer term, in positioning it for further regional expansion and national presence. The move also proved fortuitous when longtime St. Louis-based banks Centerre Bancorporation, Boatmen's Bancshares and Mercantile were acquired by out-of-state banks in the wave of consolidation in the 1990s, leaving Commerce as the only Missouri-based bank among the five largest financial institutions in the city.

One local business leader attracted to Commerce after the St. Louis banks were taken over was John Capps, whose family has extensive real estate and automotive interests in the region and a long history as St. Louis-area benefactors. He and his family moved their banking to Commerce after Boatmen's Bancshares was acquired because he wanted to do business with a bank that had proven its long-term commitment to the community.

"The national banks had people from out of town," Capps said. "They were not St. Louis natives. You knew they were here for a finite period of time." Capps was impressed enough with the Kempers and Commerce to become a member of the bank's board of directors.

Today, in the number of physical offices and by financial measures such as total deposits, the bank is approximately the same size in St. Louis as it is in Kansas City. Thirty years after making his home in the St. Louis area, David Kemper continues to live there, and Commerce executives and employees at all levels are deeply involved in St. Louis-area service, arts, civic and charitable organizations.

The February 1983 issue of Corporate Report *magazine profiled James Kemper, Jr. and three of his children— left to right, Laura, Jonathan and David, all of whom worked for the bank at the* time. The article concluded, "Given the family Kemper all pulling together at Commerce, the holding company could turn out to be the most powerful acquirer in the region."

Brookings Hall is the administrative nerve center of Washington University, where Commerce Chairman and CEO David Kemper has served as a trustee and board member for two decades.

An Interest in Education

Based on a belief that communities need strong educational systems in order to thrive, Commerce and the Kempers have long been involved in efforts to improve the quality of education throughout Kansas and Missouri. The initiative began when James Kemper, Jr. became a member of the University of Kansas City board in the mid-1950s and president of the Kansas City School Board in the early '60s.

In 1991, the William T. Kemper Foundation began awarding fellowships for teaching excellence at the University of Missouri, where five professors are selected every year to receive $10,000 awards. The foundation funded similar fellowships at the University of Kansas.

Kemper's sons have carried on the tradition. For the past two decades, David Kemper has served as a trustee of Washington University in St. Louis, helping the school's leadership in many ways. Washington University Chancellor Mark Wrighton credits the Kempers for providing "phenomenal" support to the university and to David Kemper as "an engaged partner" during two decades on the board of trustees, including time as board chairman.

Also in the St. Louis area, Commerce donated land to build the Julia Davis Library in the 1990s; it shares a parking lot with a Commerce Bank branch in North St. Louis. In Kansas City, Jonathan Kemper was instrumental in the relocation of the downtown Kansas City Public Library into the former headquarters of the First National Bank of Kansas City. In a $50 million project, the Kempers and Commerce Bank joined with the Hall Family Foundation, the Kauffman Foundation, the Kansas City Community Foundation and many other benefactors to provide funds and leadership to purchase and renovate that building and an adjacent parking lot that is now the location of the Library's remarkable, four-story garage known as the "Community Bookshelf," an innovative design suggested by Jonathan Kemper.

Jonathan Kemper was instrumental in helping Kansas City Public Library's new Central Library relocate to a renovated First National Bank building in 2004. The library's garage has the unique "community bookshelf" theme suggested by Kemper; he later was named to the library board of trustees, where he is now serving as president.

Jonathan and David Kemper became the fifth generation of family members to lead the bank when they assumed top management positions in the 1980s. Their roles in the decades to follow would prove significant as Commerce continued to grow by acquisition, entered new markets, developed new services and became more technologically sophisticated—all while retaining its community connections, Midwestern values and the business practices that had made it a trusted and successful institution for more than a century.

REACHING FURTHER

The 1980s brought great changes in state and national bank regulation. In 1983, Missouri changed its banking laws, permitting bank holding companies to merge banks it owned in the same county. Four years later, the state began allowing limited branch banking, and in 1991, Missouri moved to a statewide branch banking system under which resident banks could open new offices in the state virtually without restriction.

As Missouri relaxed its banking regulations, Commerce expanded its Kansas City-area reach. By 1984, Commerce had five affiliates in Jackson County, where Kansas City is located, including the newly acquired Plaza Bank of Commerce, established in the 1920s on the Country Club Plaza by the Kemper family. Within the company, these affiliates were the "Jackson Five," and they were part of a branch expansion that would continue for the next two decades.

A push toward interstate banking was also underway. Regional banking laws by 1984 allowed banks in New England and the Southeast to span state lines. That year, David Kemper testified before Missouri legislators, urging them to allow the state's banks to similarly acquire banks in surrounding states to prevent the largest national banks from swallowing up the major Missouri banks. "We have in this regional banking concept a tremendous opportunity for job creation in St. Louis and Kansas City," he said. "On the other hand, national banking would clearly be a threat to that employment base."

Responding to this logic, Missouri passed a law in 1986 that allowed Missouri banks to purchase banks in surrounding states and banks in surrounding states to buy banks in Missouri. Because of its longstanding correspondent banking operation, Commerce had relationships with many banks in Kansas, and it made its first acquisition

Quick Reversal in St. Joseph

Commerce Bank's acquisition of First National Bank of St. Joseph, Missouri, in 1985 not only represented a significant addition to the bank's expanding operation at the time, it offered a glimpse into how significantly the industry changed in just a few years.

The acquisition took place eight years after the Federal Reserve had denied Commerce's proposed purchase of a majority stake in another St. Joseph bank because Commerce already owned one bank in the city. In 1977, a time when the industry was quite healthy, Commerce wanted to purchase 52 percent of the shares of Farmers State Bank, but the Fed turned the bank down, saying the transaction would have "adverse effects" on the market by concentrating too much business in the hands of one bank. At the time, Farmers State held $13.3 million in deposits and Commerce Bank of St. Joseph had $39.9 million.

Only three years later, there began a run of the greatest number of bank failures in the United States since the Depression. More than 1,600 FDIC-insured banks failed between 1980 and 1994. One of them was the First National Bank of St. Joseph, founded in 1894, which became the fifth Missouri bank to fail in 1985 (and the largest since the 1930s). The U.S. Comptroller of the Currency ordered it closed on Friday, October 11, after a large number of agriculture loans went bad. With the government's assistance, Commerce acquired the much larger bank, paying about $71 million for First National and its $144 million in deposits. The acquisition gave Commerce a far larger share of the market than a Farmers State acquisition would have eight years earlier.

Interestingly, James Kemper, Jr. recalled that his colleagues at Commerce had to convince the federal regulators who were present at First National on the day it was closed to allow them to enter the bank so

9.35.02.

that, following the acquisition, they could re-open as a Commerce Bank branch as soon as possible the following Monday. What was the hurry? "I didn't want the customers to move all their business to another bank," Kemper said.

When Commerce purchased the First National Bank of St. Joseph, Missouri, in 1985, it acquired the bank's historic downtown building, which was constructed in 1902.

outside Missouri in 1992 when it completed the purchase of the First National Bank of Bonner Springs, Kansas. The agreement was announced in 1991, and the transaction was completed the following year when Kansas passed legislation allowing interstate banking.

In the midst of the savings and loan crisis of the late 1980s and early '90s, federal regulators took over hundreds of failed S&Ls and placed individual branches and their related deposits in an auction for purchase by qualified healthy banks. The auctioned banks included Missouri's Blue Valley Savings & Loan Association; Commerce acquired Blue Valley branches in St. Joseph and Independence, paying $810,000 for the two physical bank branches and their $190 million in deposits.

The U.S. Congress finally approved interstate banking in 1994. In the period between 1994 and 1998, Commerce bought 16 banks in Illinois and Kansas, including major banks such as People's Bank in Bloomington, Illinois, and Union Bancshares in Wichita, Kansas. Just as it had two decades earlier, when it identified acquisition partners in Missouri, Commerce focused on growing communities where the banks operated with competent local management teams and sound philosophies.

A MULTI-STATE OPERATION

As the 1980s closed, the bank's strategy and performance garnered national media attention. It had doubled its earnings in the second half of the decade, and its assets topped $10 billion by 1989. That year, a survey by *United States Banker* rated Commerce the "least risky" and "best" bank in the country. Commerce earned that title again in 1990.

With the bank's finances and management on solid footings, James Kemper, Jr. retired as chairman in 1991. David and Jonathan were in place to manage the bank—David as chairman and CEO and Jonathan as vice chairman.

A defining element of its success in this period was the bank's determination to avoid the transactions sponsored by Wall Street brokers who were issuing large amounts

Long-term relationships are the heart of Commerce's success. Labconco Corporation in Kansas City has banked with Commerce for more than 40 years; above, from left, Pat Anderson, president; Steve Gound, chairman; and Jeff Stanton, vice president of finance. In St. Louis, Commerce has provided banking service to the Donald Danforth Plant Science Center since 1998; left, Hal Davies, chief financial officer and vice president of finance, with Sam Fiorello, COO.

Commerce expanded into Illinois and the Wichita, Kansas, market in the 1990s. Four years after the First National Bank of Peoria celebrated its 125th anniversary, above, Commerce acquired the bank along with three other First National Bank branches in Illinois. Commerce entered the Wichita market in 1995 and constructed its multi-tenant headquarters in the city's Waterfront shopping and business district in 2005.

of high-yield debt for leveraged buyouts. Reflecting his aversion to this "junk bond" craze, David Kemper wrote a satirical piece for *The New Republic,* proposing that America could get rich by conducting a leveraged buyout of itself and then recapitalizing by auctioning off the area west of the Mississippi to the Japanese and/or the Sultan of Brunei (some people thought he was serious). He did suggest that Minneapolis and St. Paul be kept together in the retained portion for the benefit of major-league sports.

Now a multi-state business, Commerce Bancshares needed to ensure that its management and operations reflected the bank's greater size and complexity. The bank reevaluated its operations at the beginning of the 1990s in an effort to improve internal processes and customer service.

Inside the bank, changes were made to ensure future growth and profitability, with a major strategic effort called "Tomorrow's Bank." Commerce reviewed its operations for ways to cut costs and be more efficient. The work resulted

in two significant initiatives: one to improve and centralize certain back-room processing operations, the other to develop and adopt a formal mission statement.

Sara Foster, as a supervisor and later director of human resources for the bank's St. Louis region, was active in developing the new mission statement. "We used the idea of customer focus to bring everybody together" toward shared goals, Foster said.

The new mission statement made a single question— "Does it help the customer?"—Commerce's guiding principle for making decisions. That idea evolved by the late 1990s into the statement "Be Accessible, Offer Solutions, Build Relationships" and, more recently, a singular focus on customer service through consultative selling: "Ask Listen Solve." In the meantime, Commerce took steps to bring employees into the ranks of company ownership and to empower them to do their best work. In 1987, Commerce adopted an employee stock ownership program (ESOP)

Commerce
Bank
**Welcomes
President
Clinton**
JUNE 14, 1994

President Bill Clinton announced his 1994 plan for welfare reform in an address in Commerce's Walnut Lobby, taking the occasion to recognize the bank's participation in "welfare-to-work" programs and calling the city a "good place to honor work." Jonathan Kemper is seated at the far right on the stage.

and a participating investment plan (PIP) through which employees purchased about 3 percent of the outstanding shares of Commerce stock. The Kemper family put some of its shares into the ESOP, and for seven years—until the plan was fully subscribed—participating employees received an allocation of shares based on a percentage of their salaries. The last allocation was made in 1994, and the ESOP was merged into the PIP.

Not wanting to focus on only financial metrics and believing it crucial to understand its performance relative to two of its most important constituencies, Commerce adopted a "balanced scorecard" to join its goals for revenue and profit with its performance in employee engagement and customer satisfaction. The bank initiated a program of annual employee surveys to gauge whether employees are

motivated, whether the company inspires them to do their best work and whether they believe strongly in Commerce Bank's values and goals. The bank has achieved scores of 90 percent favorable or higher in both the employee and customer surveys every year since 2009.

It was important to Commerce, especially in a tightening labor market, that the best people choose Commerce as a place to work and that the bank and its customers benefit from those employees' growing experience and knowledge. After all, said Jonathan Kemper, "The best business knowledge is not in manuals and memos; it's in people's heads. What makes a bank is its people, and we know we have to work hard to hold on to them in the future."

Commerce provided employees with "Big Picture" training in the mid-2000s to help ensure that they are connected and accountable to one another and to customers. From left: Siva Ramaswamy, business intelligence analyst; Diane Kroner, employee relations manager; Diana Bentz, senior organizational development consultant; Mark French, contact center supervisor; Jeannie Ford, administrative assistant; and Corey Cotton, financial services representative. Opposite, Commerce issues a report on its community-support activities every year.

GETTING STRONGER

While the U.S. economy grew steadily from the early 1980s until the start of the 21st century, there were bumps along the way. The savings and loan crisis that began with the removal of interest rate controls in the early 1980s led to the failure of nearly a third of the nation's S&Ls by 1995, ultimately because of bad real estate loans. In the early days of the Internet and the "sub-prime" housing bubble, which burst in 2008, some banks again loosened their standards.

Commerce Bank did not participate in making the kind of risky loans that would later cause pain to many bankers. Commerce generally had avoided lending to technology companies, which were heavily promoted but typically had little track record, no history of generating profits and, in many cases, little or no revenue. The bank's caution was validated when the dot-com bubble started to burst in March 2000; more than half of all the Internet-based companies were out of business by 2004.

Every year, more than 2,000 critically ill or injured people from around Illinois are sped by Order of St. Francis HealthCare's helicopters to regional referral centers and Level 1 trauma centers in Peoria and Rockford. To help OSF HealthCare upgrade its fleet in 2012, Commerce Bank purchased four new helicopters and leased them to OSF HealthCare, one of the nation's largest privately operated aeromedical programs.

LiFE

STANDING FIRM ON RISK

The lending tradition that began with Dr. Woods remained rigorous, and while Commerce forewent short-term earnings, its standards and good reputation remained intact when the dust from the Internet and housing crises settled. Commerce won business from customers who wanted to work with banks they trusted, and it stayed healthy enough to raise its dividend while banks with large Internet portfolios struggled. In fact, when others were cutting back during these troubled periods, Commerce was hiring employees in its commercial bank and trust businesses.

During his time building Commerce, James Kemper, Jr. personally passed on his philosophy of best lending practices, ensuring that the next generation of Commerce bankers understood where the bank stood on acceptable risks. Many of today's Commerce executives say they learned how to judge good credit from bad by watching him work with customers and in the bank's loan committees.

"I never want to send in the Marines to collect our loans," Kemper frequently said, and he felt it essential that Commerce's loan officers instinctively discern when the circumstances called for saying "no." One Commerce executive remembered a textbook example from James Kemper, Jr.'s tenure. When, in the 1960s and early 1970s, other banks were making loans to quickly growing Latin American countries, Commerce refrained, fearing the countries' economic growth unsustainable and that the loans would go bad. Indeed, Latin American debt levels skyrocketed to $315 billion—or more than 50 percent of the region's gross domestic product—by 1983. As the price of oil rose, those countries were faced with rising costs and were unable to repay their loans.

Commerce's Edge training represents the bank's effort to consciously maintain and shape the corporate culture to ensure innovation and success in today's increasingly dynamic and competitive environment. Left, Tom Noack, Commerce's general counsel, participates in an Edge breakout session with Greg Nickle, enterprise operations manager, at left. Above, Steve Byrne, director of Commerce's corporate facilities, oversaw Project Green to upgrade energy and environmental systems, including replacement of the 25-year-old air-conditioning equipment at Commerce's headquarters, substantially lowering energy costs.

Cereal Food Processors' founder Fred Merrill, Sr. poses in front of one of the company's flour sifters at Cereal Food's Kansas City, Kansas, flour mill. Commerce partnered with Merrill as an initial equity investor in the company in 1972, and the bank has remained a key partner to Cereal Foods, providing credit and treasury services that supported the company's growth into the nation's largest independent flour miller.

The bank's lending discipline was not only the result of its legacy of best practices. Commerce also went beyond traditional accounting in training its loan officers, teaching them how to value assets and manage risk consistent with a philosophy of taking the long view and not being unduly influenced by short-term profits.

A DIFFERENT WAY OF INVESTING IN BUSINESSES

Another hallmark of Commerce's strategy is how it invests in businesses as an equity partner. By the early 2000s, ComTrusCo, an operation formed by Commerce in 1958 to invest in growth-stage businesses, had been succeeded by a similar entity called Capital for Business, which had equity investments in nearly 100 companies.

Originally, Capital for Business was intended to be a higher-risk program through which the bank would loan money to companies that didn't meet Commerce's standard lending qualifications, but in 1982 David Kemper shifted its business model to that of private-equity investment specializing in smaller to medium-sized manufacturing and distribution companies. With an investment philosophy similar to that of Commerce's approach to credit, Capital for Business provides longer-term support for stable businesses seeking to reach their next stage of growth or to support transfers of ownership, often to incumbent management. In these situations, Capital for Business typically acquires majority or substantial minority stakes in its portfolio companies.

In the early 2000s, Capital for Business started working with customers across the country that needed financing for a variety of purposes: transitioning to new ownership, starting a new life following a spinoff from a larger company, expanding geographically, entering new markets or developing new products. It's a fast-paced business that requires investment managers to know the industries they're investing in and to be able to accurately assess risk.

"We are trying to provide value for customers at all levels, and we have to be there when the customers are ready," said Stephen Broun, managing partner of Capital for Business since 2007.

Reflecting Commerce's long-term orientation—and its commitment to supporting the health of its communities—one of Capital for Business' core principles is that it will not invest in or purchase companies that plan to substantially reduce employment or focus on short-term gains to the detriment of long-term viability.

Cereal Food Processors Inc. (CFP), the nation's largest independent flour milling company, is a good example. Fred Merrill, Sr. founded the company in 1972 by acquiring a flour mill in Cleveland, with Capital for Business providing part of the financing and taking an equity stake. The following year, Commerce Bank loaned CFP money to expand. The loan was paid off in 10 years, but Capital for Business maintained its minority ownership until the company was sold in 2014.

"The company's performance was very good," said Broun. "They were a highly valued bank customer, and when management determined it was the right time to sell the company, it turned out favorably for CFP and very well for us."

Today, with manufacturing beginning to return to American shores from the Far East, Commerce is positioning Capital for Business to support companies committed to making products in the United States.

CREDIT CARD STRATEGY

The same kind of disciplined attention Commerce paid to risk in its commercial lending and private-equity businesses also paid dividends in credit cards. Commerce had continually adapted to changing market conditions—almost always with success—since entering the credit card business in 1964, and in the early 2000s, Commerce adopted a new strategic plan for the business. It called for deliberate growth and keeping a watchful eye on the economy.

Toward the end of 2007, Commerce began to see an increase in delinquent credit card accounts, which was a

The transportation-infrastructure engineering firm HNTB, founded in Kansas City, is a longtime Commerce customer that has grown with the bank's support to more than 60 offices nationwide. From left are former HNTB President Ken Graham, Executive Chairman Harvey Hammond, Executive Vice President Paul Yarossi, former Southeast Division President Kevin McDonald and former Executive Vice President Ed McSpedon.

recession hit in 2008, Commerce did not; though its profits declined, its credit card operation continued to be profitable. Many consumers began more carefully managing their debt, and Commerce worked with them to achieve their financial goals.

Today, credit and debit cards represent one of the bank's fastest-growing and most profitable businesses and one where Commerce has established an outsized presence: while Commerce is the 37th largest U.S. bank in assets, it is one of the top 20 banks in the card business.

DECLINING TARP

The housing market was at the center of the economic turmoil that struck Wall Street, and then Main Street, beginning in the spring of 2008. Lenders and loan brokers, in a sometimes frenzied bid to increase the number of loans sold to Wall Street, had been extending mortgage credit to homeowners who might not have qualified for a loan under normal criteria—the so-called sub-prime borrowers who had inadequate credit histories, income and/ or collateral value. These lenders then sold many of those loans to other financial institutions, removing the obligations from their books and freeing themselves to originate more of these questionable loans. Many large banks and investment houses packaged the loans into securities, sold them to investors and then often created derivatives underpinned by those dodgy loan packages.

This house of cards remained standing until foreclosures on U.S. homes increased dramatically in 2006 and 2007—and with the underlying real estate values falling, the value of the mortgages, the value and liquidity of the collateral-backed securities and the value of the derivative securities plummeted. A dozen major banks and many other financial institutions filed for bankruptcy court protection or went out

Tony Clayton, president of Missouri-based Clayton Agri-Marketing, Inc., turned to Commerce for international banking, credit card and treasury services to transport livestock. The payoff of providing trusted service to companies like his helped Commerce achieve second place on Bank Director *magazine's 2006 scorecard of the nation's top-performing banks. The magazine's fourth-quarter issue that year, right, noted that "Commerce is very good at most things ... highly profitable, with a strong balance sheet and excellent loan quality."*

precursor to problems that would soon reveal themselves throughout the greater economy. In an attempt to understand the trend, senior managers of Commerce's credit card operation kept in close communication with their collectors, who told them that many consumers were increasingly unable to keep up with their debt. Commerce changed its card acquisition strategy, minimizing offers of new credit to consumers who might be already overextended and generally managing credit limits to assure that individual lines could be handled responsibly. This helped maintain charge-off levels below industry averages. More important, while most of the credit card industry lost money when the

of business. To avert widespread economic collapse and, many feared, a depression as catastrophic as the one in the 1930s, the federal government pumped $700 billion in stimulus spending into the economy and spent billions more propping up banks, investment houses, insurers and other financial institutions that had suffered big losses.

Commerce Bancshares was not one of them, as for the most part it had shunned the riskier classes of real estate-backed securities and declined to make sub-prime mortgages in its communities. "We were about the only bank of size in the country not to own these things," David Kemper said. With stocks falling, money market funds in trouble and a number of big and small banks failing, customers who sought safety and soundness turned to Commerce to deposit their funds. Between 2008 and 2012, Commerce experienced record deposit growth of $5.5 billion, or 42 percent.

Through the Troubled Asset Relief Program, or TARP, the U.S. government purchased assets and equity from financial institutions to shore up the financial sector. Many banks that were not at risk of failing accepted TARP money to boost reserves and stabilize their balance sheets. With the urging of some regulators and rating agencies, Commerce executives discussed whether to become involved in the TARP program and decided against it, determining it basically wasn't right—its reputation was sound, its business wasn't in trouble and its prudent lending practices had insulated the bank from concentrations of bad loans. As it turned out, Commerce was the country's third largest bank to decline the government's assistance.

"We believed that it was more of a financial panic and not a problem at our company," David Kemper explained. "That turned out to be true. Our basic assessment was that we didn't need any handouts from the government."

Chuck Kim, chief financial officer of Commerce Bancshares, said it would have been out of character for Commerce to accept TARP funds: "One of the things that I thought was that we ran our bank for more than 140 years

Chairman and CEO David Kemper testified before a key U.S. House of Representatives' subcommittee in February 2011 about the serious implications of the Durbin Amendment to the Dodd-Frank banking legislation passed the prior year, which set federal price controls on debit card transactions.

Commerce Bank's data center staff monitors transactions, business applications and hardware for optimal performance 24 hours a day. Based on a comprehensive framework of service levels and severity indicators, the bank has set response times for addressing and escalating issues that might impair the system's stability and security.

in a certain way so that we don't have to take TARP."

To be sure, some Commerce loans went into default and on a few occasions required foreclosure, but Commerce's strategy of prudently assessing risk allowed it to survive and sustain its customer relationships while many other financial institutions struggled (and some sank).

BRINGING ON ANOTHER GENERATION

David Kemper's son, John W. Kemper, was not initially drawn to the banking industry. A 2000 graduate of Stanford University, with advanced degrees from the London School

of Economics and Northwestern University, John Kemper took a job with a tech startup after graduating from Stanford and then worked as a consultant for McKinsey & Company for five years. In 2007, he came back to St. Louis and joined Commerce as director of strategic planning to help identify growth strategies.

At the time, the economic outlook in the country was still rosy, but it wasn't long before John was faced with helping the bank make it through the recession. "It was an uncertain and at times scary period in the financial industry, but we also saw it as a time of opportunity," he said. "We

The 2011 Tornado

When the most costly tornado in U.S. history struck Joplin, Missouri, on May 22, 2011, killing more than 150 people, two Commerce Bank branches were destroyed: one across from Mercy Hospital Joplin and another on East 20th Street, where the only structure left standing was the vault. The bank and its employees in Joplin were relatively fortunate, however. Although some employees were left temporarily homeless, no one suffered serious injury. Had the storm struck on any day but a Sunday, with the bank's three branches in Joplin open, things could have been much worse.

Commerce quickly opened a makeshift branch to help customers with tasks such as signing up for new debit cards to replace those lost in the disaster. Employees donated more than $50,000 to some of their Joplin colleagues to help them get back on their feet.

"One of the highlights of my career was to see all that happen," said Mike Petrie, a senior vice president at Commerce and director of community bank administration. "That defines Commerce. It's a people business, and we have the best people around."

Interestingly, not long after the weather cleared, employees from both branches went to their workplaces to sift through the rubble to find the $350,000 that had been in teller drawers. When they were done, only 26 cents was unaccounted for. Petrie offered to make that up out of his pocket, but his employees refused to allow it, reminding him that it was against company policy.

After a deadly tornado struck Joplin, Missouri, in May 2011, Commerce Bank employees jumped into action. They scrambled to open a temporary branch, left, to replace the one that had been destroyed, and they secured money that had been locked in teller drawers. Above, a sign of commitment to the Joplin community was placed on the bank's vault—the only structure in the branch that survived the tornado.

had plenty to lend and a philosophy of extending credit that didn't change. In times like that, customers see what a partner bank is really made of." In 2013, Kemper was named president and chief operating officer of Commerce Bancshares. John Capps, a member of Commerce Bancshares' board, credits John Kemper with bringing "a new understanding and a new energy" to the bank.

In order to prepare the next generation of leaders, the bank has been developing its management team with a combination of deep experience and new blood. Charles Kim oversees strategic planning and marketing as well as the retail side of the business. Ray Stranghoener, with the bank since 1999, oversees the trust business.

After joining Commerce in 1984, Kevin Barth appreciates the bank's strategy of moving executives around to various jobs to give them a breadth of experience to drawn upon. Over a 30-year career, Barth became president and chief operating officer of the Kansas City bank and

then Commerce Bancshares' executive vice president of commercial lending—a position from which he is helping push the bank's expansion into new geographic markets.

Jeff Burik oversees the commercial card and payments business, which he is leading into a variety of new markets. Sara Foster, as the bank's executive vice president, chief human resources officer and director of internal support services, meets evolving skills needs and keeps pace with contemporary thinking in employee advancement, retention and succession planning. The Leadership Development Program, which Foster began at the bank in 2004, focuses on identifying potential future leaders.

At the core of every successful financial institution is a sound and prudent credit policy, and in 2010, Dan Callahan stepped into a role previously held by bank legends Arthur Eisenhower and Harry Wuerth when he became senior vice president of Commerce Bancshares, chief credit officer and chief risk officer. Commerce's strong culture helped ease

Teamwork has always been a hallmark of Commerce's way of doing business, internally as well as externally. From left, Alyssa Franzke, Tami Nugent, Marc Christman, Jared Robinson and Adam House collaborate on approaches to help Commerce's commercial customers implement efficient new payment solutions.

the transition from Bob Matthews to Callahan in the midst of an economic downturn, and Callahan has shown strong leadership in lending and credit while providing the bank with steady oversight and discipline.

Recognizing that technology has important human and cultural dimensions in large organizations, Robert Rauscher, who joined the bank in 1980 and was named a senior vice president of Commerce Bancshares and director of operations and information services in 1997, was called upon to lead a culture-shaping initiative called Edge. The initiative focuses on joint investments in people and technology in order to meet evolving customer needs

and support Commerce's products while increasing revenue and improving profitability.

The increasingly high-tech, interconnected and interdependent world is changing as quickly for Commerce as it is for every other business, and Commerce's new leadership team operates on the belief that future success depends on innovation, teamwork and growth based on its traditional core values. As Barth said, one of Commerce's chief reasons for success has been its ability to take "what we've learned over 150 years and bring those values to new opportunities and markets, to add value and compete effectively."

As Commerce turns 150, it is carrying its heritage forward while testing new ideas, including, as shown here, the Vandeventer "branch of the future" in St. Louis. Opposite, Jennifer Scherffius, a small-business banking officer, and Valerie Shaw, head of retail administration in the Central Missouri region, are among the employees who will carry the bank into the future.

FUTURE COMMERCE

A s Commerce Bank celebrates in 150th year in business, it is still independent and still Missouri–based, although its 350 offices now reach across the central United States and Texas from Ohio and Tennessee through to the front range of the Rocky Mountains. The bank is a subsidiary of the holding company Commerce Bancshares, Inc., and its portfolio of financial services includes business and personal banking, wealth management, and estate planning and investments. It has subsidiaries in mortgage banking, credit-related insurance, private equity and real estate activities. As of this writing, Commerce had more than 4,700 employees.

Commerce has managed the investment assets of the University of Central Missouri (UCM) in Warrensburg since 1991. Between 2009 and 2014, with guidance from Commerce, the University's endowed funds grew from $30 million to $51 million—even after more than $18 million was distributed to UCM for scholarships and other mission-critical needs. Five-year investment returns have placed UCM in the top quartile of institutional endowments nationwide, as reported by the National Association of College and University Business Officers rankings.

"LET THEM WORK AND MAKE YOU MONEY"

Commerce has been recognized as one of the strongest and best-performing banks in the country over time. It has raised its regular cash dividend every year for 47 consecutive years, and since 1984, its stock price has increased by more than 2,300 percent. Over that same period, the NASDAQ Bank Index has risen 1,148 percent and the Standard & Poor's 500 index 1,231 percent. Over a 10-year period ending in 2014, Commerce's annualized total shareholder return was 6.2 percent; that compares to 0.6 percent for NASDAQ bank stocks in aggregate. In 2014, Commerce Bancshares' assets of $24 billion placed the company 37th among U.S. banks, and a market capitalization of $4.2 billion ranked Commerce 31st among U.S. banks. Commerce reported $262 million in net income in 2014, for a return on average common equity of 11.65 percent. That same year, Commerce Bank extended $11.5 billion in loans; total deposits were $19.5 billion. As of December 31, 2014, the company's asset-management department, Commerce Trust Company, managed more than $39 billion in total client assets.

In 2011, Commerce changed its charter from a national charter to a Missouri state charter. The decision to switch was studied at great length and has produced several benefits, primarily in consistency and efficiencies between the holding company and the bank regulator.

The financial press has taken notice of the bank's stability, continuity and consistently strong performance. For six years running, Commerce Bank has been among the top 10 on *Forbes'* list of America's best publicly traded banks and thrift institutions, ranked by overall financial health (it was ninth in 2015). It also was one of 33 returning members on the 2012 KBW Bank Honor Roll of banking institutions that achieved positive earnings-per-share growth during the last decade regardless of the economic environment.

One stock analyst, Joe Stieven of St. Louis-based Stieven Capital Advisors, which invests primarily in banks and financial services companies and is a longtime investor in Commerce Bancshares, considers Commerce "one of the safest and [most] prudently run banks you can find in the United States. When you have a really good bank with a

Forbes *named Commerce one of the 10 best performing banks in the United States in 2015. Commerce has been similarly recognized in the national media and by rating services for its customer service, stability, financial performance and long-term stock appreciation.*

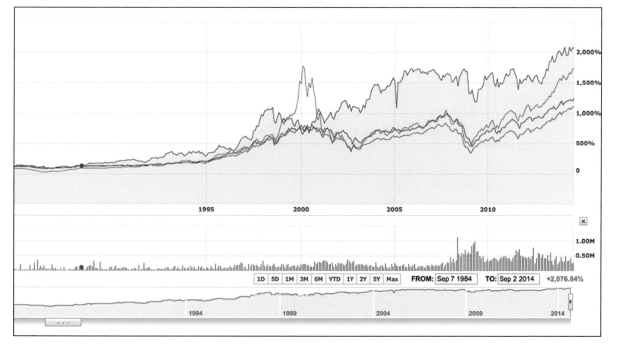

Between 1985 and 2014, Commerce's shares, represented by the blue line on the chart at left, outperformed the NASDAQ Bank Index, green line; the Dow Jones Industrial Average, red line; and Standard & Poor's 500 Index, brown line.

When AlloSource, a Colorado-based developer of tissue grafts for medical procedures, needed funding to expand its headquarters, it turned to Commerce Bank to refinance tax-exempt bonds, provide credit lines and develop a bankcard-based accounts payable program.

really good management team," he said, "our rationale is just to let them work and make you money."

For growth, Commerce Bancshares sees many opportunities as it looks ahead. With its bread-and-butter lending business and operation of branches in key Missouri markets at its core, Commerce will begin its 151st year in business with an established national presence and a focus on areas such as credit cards, payment systems and wealth management.

GROWTH IN PAYMENT SYSTEMS

Some of Commerce Bank's success over the past 90 years can be attributed to its innovative solutions to helping customers access the payments system. Commerce Bank's

efforts to provide valuable payments services can be traced back to the late 1920s, when bank representatives met rail cars loaded with checks coming into Kansas City so the bank could get them processed quickly for its customers. Those efforts evolved in the 1980s, when Commerce acquired its own ZIP codes in order to expedite collections through its lockbox operations—becoming the largest customer of the U.S. Postal Service in Kansas City.

Building on its expertise in credit card processing, Commerce continued to develop its payments system through the end of the 20th century and into the 21st. The bank is now one of the nation's 35 largest issuers of consumer and commercial card products, according to data collected by the Nilson Report as of 2014.

Commerce began offering consumer credit cards in the late 1960s and became a national leader in helping its retail customers conduct transactions electronically. In the 1980s, Commerce was the first to make credit and debit transactions possible via the same card—the Special Connections card. In the 1990s, Commerce introduced a variety of debit cards, including some of the country's first University Cards, which give students access to campus services and their Commerce Bank accounts via a single ID card. In the first decade of the 2000s, Commerce expanded its consumer card territory, and today it processes more than $6.5 billion worth of consumer credit and debit card transactions a year.

COMMERCIAL PAYMENTS

The bank added to its growing consumer credit card business by expanding into commercial card payments in the 1980s. Today, Commerce is a major servicer for converting commercial customers' paper checks to electronic payments, which are then applied directly to the vendors' accounts receivable. Commerce developed this card-based payment solution to help its commercial customers make efficient, accurate and cost-effective payments. "Paying bills is not a skill set that most people go into business for," said Jeff Burik, senior vice president of commercial card and merchant services. "But companies do have to pay their bills. They either hire people to do it in-house, or they have a vendor do it for them. That is the future of payments."

For example, businesses can buy and sell products or services from one another, leveraging Commerce Bank as the billing and payment conduit. Whether the initial invoice is paper or electronic, all invoices are routed electronically for approval. If buyer and seller agree on the invoice amount, Commerce will pay the seller immediately upon approval of the invoice, minus a small fee for the privilege of receiving the payment early; the buyer then pays Commerce the full amount of the invoice on its original due date. This allows sellers to receive payment sooner, while buyers keep

their money until the original invoice due date. Commerce receives the fee deducted from the original invoice amount, generating new revenues and short-term loan business for the bank.

These relationships have been strongest during periods of uncertainty when Commerce experienced large inflows of deposits, as companies sought to protect balances above FDIC-insured levels, seeking the safety and soundness of Commerce. In order to respond to this growing business, Commerce has hired a dedicated staff to run this operation for its more than 1,000 commercial card customers.

In addition to making credit card transactions more efficient, Commerce has developed innovative payment services for specific industries such as health care, and it is one of the few banks in the country in this business. As of early 2015, Commerce was partnering with approximately 100 hospitals in the United States to help patients finance their bills; the average bill financed through this system is

Commerce provides a range of customized payment-systems services, tools and technology to support the unique needs of the health care industry. Above, from left, Julie Krueger, commercial small business marketing manager; Rob Bratcher, commercial banking manager, Kansas City; and Jeff Fahler, treasury services sales manager, Kansas City, review marketing materials. Commerce Bank's Visa card, opposite, has become the platform for a multitude of payments products the bank offers to individual and business customers.

Lifelong and devoted Kansas Citians, the Bloch family has done its banking with Commerce for four generations. Commerce helped brothers Henry and Richard Bloch start their business in 1955 and grow it into H&R Block, the world's largest tax preparation service company. The Bloch family has also been a leader in many civic and cultural causes in its hometown, including the Nelson-Atkins Museum of Art, where, above, Henry Bloch and his son, Tom, converse in the new Bloch Building, endowed by the Bloch family.

about $2,500, although loan amounts can be as high as $50,000.

Burik said this business fits well into Commerce's payment systems operation because the bank excels at handling smaller charges and a large volume of transactions. As Burik explained, "You go where the fish are. Credit is going to be needed there."

The commercial payments business serves important market needs for rapid processing of financial transactions and greater certainty in collection while, in the case of health care, solving the vexing consumer problem of paying for large and unexpected expenses.

Commerce chose to develop the expertise, set up an infrastructure and offer a payments service to clients because an increasing number of large companies preferred to focus on their core business rather than manage the increasingly complex process of paying bills and collecting money from their customers. Chuck Kim, Commerce's chief financial officer, said that, in addition to offering good growth potential, the commercial payments business is profitable and relatively low-risk.

Commercial payments relationships have been a steady source of fee income and strong core deposits for Commerce. The company's commercial card revenue rose to $88 million in 2014—more than double the revenue of 2009, and as of 2014, the bank was processing more than $6 billion worth of transactions for its commercial card clients. Commercial payments contributed $275 million, or 63 percent, of the bank's net income in 2014, a more than 20 percent increase over 2005. Commerce expects the payments business to grow well into the future as more of the economy shifts to electronic payments.

FULL-SERVICE WEALTH MANAGEMENT

Investment management for individuals, institutions and businesses has been a staple of Commerce's business dating back to its founding. Traditionally, Commerce Bank was known for its strength in proprietary fixed-income

management, conservative equity investing and highly personalized service for families and institutional clients.

At the time Commerce bought County Tower Bank in the early 1980s, it had no trust or asset management operation outside the Kansas City area. To expand the business statewide, Commerce hired bankers and wealth management executives who knew the bank's other Missouri communities. This allowed Commerce to provide trust and asset management services across the state while strengthening capabilities in markets it was already serving.

By the late 1990s, it became apparent that baby-boom demographics were driving a significant increase in the demand for wealth management advice. David Kemper decided to invest in an expansion of Commerce's wealth management business, starting with a new leadership team with experience from much larger wealth management firms.

Hired as president of Commerce Trust Company, the bank's asset management department, Ray Stranghoener was given the challenge in 1999 of increasing the bank's range of wealth management offerings while maintaining its focus on individual client relationships and personalized service. Over the next 10 years, Commerce made significant investments in professional staff, product development and technology to support this growth initiative. Commerce Trust added private banking, financial planning, tax return preparation, real estate management, family business consulting and expanded brokerage services, among others, to its portfolio of wealth management services.

Commerce Trust also made changes in its investment management services. Like most bank-owned money managers, Commerce Trust traditionally offered primarily its own home-grown investment products, including proprietary mutual funds that were created in 1994. Beginning in the early 2000s, Commerce Trust became an early leader among bank-affiliated advisors in converting from exclusively offering proprietary investment products to an "open architecture" approach to investing. This helped

Commerce arranged the bridge financing to restore and completely update the St. Louis Public Library upon its 100th anniversary in 2012. Commerce had previously created an investment policy for the library's endowment and introduced credit cards to the library's operations. In the 2012 transaction, Commerce issued private bonds structured to be repaid as scheduled donations came in to the library. From left are Rick Simoncelli, president of the St. Louis Public Library Foundation; Waller McGuire, executive director of the St. Louis Public Library; and William Jackson, the library's chief financial officer. Earl and Myrtle Walker of St. Louis, above, chose Commerce for services that include private banking, managing family foundation assets and commercial banking for their business, Carr Lane Manufacturing Company.

the client develop an individualized policy for investment and asset allocation and build a portfolio of best-in-class, third-party managers who specialize in various areas of the market.

In 2012, Commerce Trust created a new, specialized division called Commerce Family Office, which reports to John Handy, head of the private client business, and serves its growing list of very wealthy, multi-generational families with complex needs. These family-office clients typically need strategic advice and a broader range of administrative services than Commerce's core private clients. At the same time, guided by the executive team, including Scott Boswell, head of institutional client business, Commerce Trust has continued to expand its services for institutional clients, including retirement

plans, foundations, endowments and governmental entities.

As a result of all these changes, Commerce Trust is recognized as a major, full-service wealth management provider. In 2015, it ranked 26th among all national providers, based on assets under management. Between 1999 and 2014, assets under Commerce's management increased from $10 billion to $39 billion, and Commerce Trust Company's asset management fees have grown over that time from $57 million to more than $114 million.

"PEOPLE I WANTED TO BE ASSOCIATED WITH"

After Commerce expanded into Kansas and Illinois in the 1990s, it began to explore expansion into geographically contiguous areas that had growing communities and positive business climates. Though its growth was slow and methodical compared to the rest of the industry, Commerce was highly successful in integrating its acquisitions because it focused on banks with management styles and cultures similar to its own.

In 2007, Commerce acquired Commerce Bank of Colorado, a bank with $124 million in assets that was attractive because of its history of sound management. There was no previous connection between the two Commerce Banks; the fact that they had the same name was a happy bonus. The banks' management teams first explored the idea of a union in 2005, and executives spent two years getting to know one another and growing comfortable with a merger. Jim Lewien, who was chief executive officer of Commerce of Colorado, said his bank received other offers but chose Commerce Bancshares because of the relationship it had developed with Commerce's Bayard Clark, Kevin Barth and David Kemper. "They were clearly the kind of people and the type of bank that I wanted to be associated with," Lewien said.

The Colorado bank's staff, however, was initially apprehensive when the deal was announced. They had seen other Colorado banks purchased and their employees let go. Lewien, who retained his position after the merger, and Commerce Bancshares executives reassured them that Commerce Bancshares wanted them to stay and to grow the bank without radical changes in mission, identity or personnel.

"Commerce Bancshares was very, very sensitive to having the conversion be a two-way street," said Lewien. "We had a dialogue about how we would go about merging the two banks. I think that was a key factor in the success of our merger."

One of the results of that dialogue was that, in choosing which of the banks' systems and processes to retain after the merger, the banks evaluated one another's practices and agreed to use the best ones, regardless of which bank had originated them. Commerce Bancshares adopted Commerce Bank of Colorado's technology for the electronic processing

Denver's historic Union Station neighborhood is being redeveloped into a world-class, transit-oriented retail, office and residential complex. Commerce Bank provided the construction financing for the new home of IMA Financial Group, a diversified financial services company located there.

of checks and documents turned in at a teller counter.

Since the transaction closed in July 2007, Commerce's business in Colorado has grown every year, even during the recession. Commerce Bank in Colorado has tripled in size, and Lewien expects it to continue its growth at a steady pace. The merger offers a template for how Commerce plans to continue its long-held approach to growth by acquisition.

TREATING PEOPLE "THE WAY WE WANT TO BE TREATED"

Commerce Bancshares moved into Oklahoma, also in 2007, by acquiring South Tulsa Financial Corporation, which operated Bank South, a two-branch bank with $115 million in loans and $104 million in deposits. Six years later, Commerce expanded further in Tulsa by acquiring Summit Bancshares, Inc., which had $207 million in loans, $232 million in deposits and branches in Tulsa and Oklahoma City. Commerce was interested in the Tulsa market primarily because of the strength of the Oklahoma economy. However, after years of serving corporate and correspondent customers there, the bank knew that the business culture was a lot like that of Missouri and Kansas. Thus, entering the contiguous state was natural for Commerce.

Bank South, established in 1998, realized after reaching $100 million in assets in the early 2000s that it would be advantageous to combine with a larger banking company that had access to greater amounts of capital and a broader set of products and services. But it may have been the Commerce culture that clinched the deal.

"We liked what Commerce stood for," said former Bank South Chief Executive Officer Carl Hudgins, who approached Commerce's Barth about a possible merger. "The super-community bank concept was very appealing to us. It was relationship banking."

In addition to providing Bank South, now Commerce Bank in Oklahoma, with deeper pockets, the transaction allowed the Oklahoma bank to offer treasury, capital markets, corporate card and merchant card services that it had been unable to provide on its own. The 2013 acquisition

of Summit further strengthened the Oklahoma operation by providing a strong source of loans to the oil, gas and other industries, said Hudgins, now chairman of Commerce Bank in Oklahoma.

Whereas other banks often cut workers in acquired branches to reduce duplication of work and to cut costs and increase profits, Commerce retained the employees gained in the Oklahoma mergers.

"All of the things we thought would happen have happened," says Hudgins. "We were successful, and there's just more firepower and boots on the ground in Oklahoma." Prior to its purchase by Commerce, Bank South reported slightly less than $1 million in net income. In 2014, its profit was more than $7 million and growing.

Wade Edmundson, who ran Summit Bank in Tulsa, said he was attracted to Commerce for many of the same reasons Bank South executives were. "The people I knew in Tulsa

and met in Kansas City at Commerce seemed sincere," he said. "You want to affiliate with someone you can be proud to associate with."

Edmundson also appreciated how Commerce treated his employees, working to find the right jobs for them within the company after the acquisition took place. Nearly two dozen received promotions, either in Tulsa or other markets. Kevin Barth said, "It's very traumatic to be acquired. We felt, let's treat these people the way we want to be treated."

CINCINNATI, NASHVILLE AND DALLAS

Acquiring banks was only one of the ways Commerce Bancshares grew in the early 2000s. It purchased a leasing company in Cincinnati in 2003 and then hired a commercial banker to build a team there beginning in 2008. It entered Nashville by opening a loan production office in 2008 and

The Future of Branch Banking

With drive-up lanes, automated teller machines and online account management, branch banking has changed significantly in the past 50 years, and Commerce Bank expects it to change even more radically in the next decade.

In November 2014, Commerce opened a high-tech branch in St. Louis that is testing technology, services and ways of interacting that could be part of how people bank in the near-term future. Walk-up stations feature tellers accessed by remote video. A technology bar with workstations allows customers to bank via web and mobile applications. A business center serves small business customers. Branch employees are neither tellers nor financial service representatives but personal bankers who can handle a variety of tasks, including providing advice.

Mark Fishel, the owner and president of Vandeventer Truck Sales in St. Louis, began using the business center as soon as it opened, not only to bank but to expand his network of contacts and make deeper connections with people in his community.

"It gives me the opportunity to meet people in line that I have seen for several years," Fishel said. "Anybody who has a swipe card can get in. We are waiting in that business lobby. You're in a casual environment. I never knew where they were from or what they did. Everybody is talking about the new bank and exchanging ideas."

Patty Kellerhals, director of retail banking, said Commerce is "very focused on what our customers want now and in the future" and is certain that "what's going to add value for the customer is going to add value to the company and for shareholders."

Because the branch is something of an experiment, Commerce expects to fine-tune it as time goes on.

"The winners of tomorrow will be those who recognize the needs of customers and embrace the right kinds of innovation," said John Kemper, president and chief operating officer of Commerce Bancshares. "We're trying some new things to see how they resonate with customers, and keeping an open mind. The future is unclear, but I think Commerce's history gives us good reason to be optimistic."

Commerce opened its next-generation banking center in St. Louis in 2014 with a ceremony highlighted by students from the St. Louis Language Immersion School. To test new delivery approaches, the branch uses technologies such as a video transaction station, a private business center accessed by bankcard, and video conferencing with loan officers, investment advisors and other financial experts.

has grown organically by offering commercial loans in that market.

"Each time, it's been about finding a market with the characteristics you like and hiring the right people," said Barth. Cincinnati and Nashville are similar in size to Kansas City and St. Louis, and both have economies that are a mix of industrial, distribution and service niches.

The commercial expansion into Nashville and Cincinnati was overseen by Seth Leadbeater, vice chairman of Commerce Bancshares and chairman and CEO of Commerce Bank's St. Louis Region, who in 25 years with the bank has steadily managed the St. Louis market and Commerce's eastern region.

As for Dallas, Commerce Bancshares opened a commercial lending office there in 2012 when it hired two up-and-coming bankers. Commerce projected it would become profitable in Dallas after three years, but the market was profitable in less than one year.

As of 2014, 20 percent of Commerce's new loans, and 10 percent of its total loans, came from these new geographic regions. Characteristically patient, Commerce plans to continue to focus on building its presence and capacities in these new markets before turning elsewhere, according to President and Chief Operating Officer John Kemper. "We will do it in a very Commerce way," he said. "We will walk before we run. It's about building relationships. It's about getting deeper in the markets where we are."

THE PEOPLE FACTOR

An important aspect of Commerce's geographic expansion is that it has provided opportunities for employees to move around inside the organization, experience new markets and new jobs, and to take on challenges they may not think they're ready for as a way to stretch their abilities and move up through the company. Examples are to be found throughout Commerce, and they include Patty Kellerhals, executive vice president and director of retail banking, who has spent her entire 38-year career working for the bank in

many different roles. She worked her way through college as a Commerce proof operator and teller and progressed to other positions—consumer lender, branch manager, sales manager—before directing Commerce's alternative delivery channels and then moving into her current position.

"One of the best things about Commerce is that we're an organization that is small enough and personal enough to recognize talent, understand what people are achieving and what they are interested in learning and doing," said Kellerhals. "We value that, appreciate that and leverage that to create a win for both the company and the employee."

Commerce is an employer of choice for many in the industry because it has continued to grow and to try new things even in tough economic times. It also offers considerable autonomy and a rewarding work environment, and it has a strong record in developing people for career advancement. As a result, the average employment tenure at Commerce is longer than that at other banks. The average bank employee in the United States stays with his or her employer for 7.75 years. At Commerce, that number is 9.6 years.

Here today.
Here tomorrow.

commercebank.com/soundness   **Commerce Bank**

As Commerce looks to the future, it knows that people will make the difference—the people who work for Commerce and the people whose lives are made better through the bank's support. Succinctly expressing the bank's longstanding commitment to its customers and its communities is the basis of Commerce's customer promise: "Here Today. Here Tomorrow."

"We're a service business," said David Kemper, "and the No. 1 asset is not on the balance sheet. We're the employer of choice because we have been expanding, been innovative, and we allow people to take risks."

Vice President Michael Robie, whose career has been rather typical of many long-term Commerce employees, provides another good example. He started as a teller in 1974 and now runs one of Commerce's largest Kansas City branches. Robie said he wouldn't want to work anywhere else, and during more than 40 years at Commerce, he has never looked for another job. "The company has a family feel," he said. "They have always been very good to me."

TRUST, LOCAL PRESENCE AND ALL THE RIGHT SERVICES

Commerce's approach to growth has allowed it to maintain its community-bank feel while enabling it to compete against larger national banks. The company's Kansas City banking operation, for example, now has customers in every state. The depth and breadth of Commerce's offerings make it attractive to those who need a large and sophisticated set of services but might prefer a bank with local presence and community values. To them, Commerce offers all of the required services plus a relationship based on familiarity, trust, sustained performance and a commitment to the health and vitality of their community.

Building Commerce remains a work in progress, a continuing effort to know and to serve the ever-changing needs of people and businesses in an increasingly fast-moving economy. Over 150 years and through six generations of family leadership, Commerce has been privileged to contribute to the well-being of its customers, its communities and its employees, and to take part in the building of America's West.

Commerce Bank's history began with the opening of the West, when a flood of pioneers first came to settle the center of the North American continent. The bronze sculpture entitled Corps of Discovery in Kansas City's Case Park at Eighth and Jefferson streets was dedicated in 2000 on the occasion of Kansas City's 150th anniversary. It honors Thomas Jefferson's prophetic vision of a continental nation, the achievements of Lewis and Clark in their heroic journey of discovery, and the lives of millions of men and women who have followed, coming to America's heartland from all corners of the world.

150 YEARS OF BUILDING COMMERCE

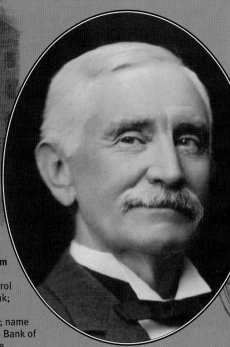

1865
Kansas City Savings Association is organized with $10,000 in capital. **Francis Long** is president.

1881
Dr. William S. Woods buys control of the bank; becomes president; name change to Bank of Commerce.

1870

1880

1890

1873
Kansas City Savings Association takes offices above the Magnolia Saloon at 4th and Delaware.

1885
Bank of Commerce moves its location to 6th and Delaware.

1887
Bank of Commerce is granted national charter; becomes National Bank of Commerce.

1893
National bank panic. National Bank of Commerce remains open and strong while more than 500 banks in U.S. fail or suspend operations.

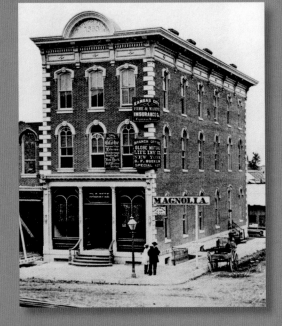

W. S. Woods, President.
F. E. Marshall, Vice Prest.

C. J. White, Cashier

H. C. Schwitzgebel, Asst Cashier
W. A. Rule, 2nd Asst Cash'r

CAPITAL $2,000,000 ºº SURPLUS $100,000 ºº

3760.

National Bank of Commerce

Kansas City Mo

2/25/94

Longan & Higgins, Attys.,

Sedalia, Mo.

Gentlemen:-

Your letter of the 21st is received, and contents noted.

If L. F. Sheldon will pay half of the

ORIENT

The Kansas City, Mexico & Orient Railroad
AND PRINCIPAL CONNECTIONS.

▬▬▬ Lines in Operation
▬ ▬ ▬ " under Construction
▬ ▬ " Proposed

1906
Commerce Trust Company is organized. **Dr. Woods** appoints **William Thornton "W.T" Kemper** vice president; work starts on 15-story building at the corner of 10th and Walnut in Kansas City, one of the tallest buildings west of the Mississippi.

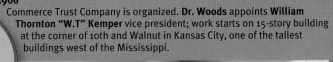

1900
National Bank of Commerce is the 12th largest bank in the U.S., with more than $36 million in deposits. **Arthur Stilwell** organizes the Kansas City, Mexico & Orient Railroad, financed in part by **Dr. Woods.**

1908
Dr. Woods regains control of the bank, recapitalizes and expunges the **Ridgelys.**

1914
Federal Reserve System is formed; with the urging of KC leaders, Missouri becomes only state with two Federal Reserve banks.

1900   **1910**

1907
Monetary panic sparked by the failure of the Knickerbocker Trust Company of New York. National Bank of Commerce is placed into receivership by **William Ridgely,** Comptroller of the Currency, who resigns his post and is appointed receiver of Commerce along with his brother.

1912
National Bank of Commerce merges with Southwest National Bank: takes name of Southwest National Bank until 1919.

1915
Commerce hosts first meeting of Federal Reserve Bank of Kansas City.

1916
Commerce Trust combines with Southwest National Bank; operates separately until 1921.

1903
Future President **Harry Truman** starts work as collector at Commerce. Housemate is another Commerce employee, **Arthur Eisenhower,** brother of future President **Dwight D. Eisenhower.**

1919
"Southwest" is dropped from the company name.

APPLICATION FOR EMPLOYMENT.

Position desired *Collector*

HISTORY, FAMILY CONNECTIONS AND REFERENCES.

NATIONAL BANK OF COMMERCE

ESTABLISHED 1865.

CAPITAL   SURPLUS
$2,000,000. $500,000.

GEO. D. FORD, Vice President.
J. J. HEIM, Vice President.
WALTER S. DISKEY, Vice President.
W. L. BUECHLE, Vice President.
W. H. SEEGER, Vice President.

J. W. PERRY, President.

CHAS. H. MOORE, Vice President.
JAS. T. BRADLEY, Cashier.
CHAS. M. VINING, Assistant Cashier.
W. H. GLASKIN, Assistant Cashier.
JAS. F. MEADE, Assistant Cashier.

150 YEARS OF BUILDING COMMERCE

1938
W.T. Kemper dies; **James Kemper, Sr.** becomes chairman of the board.

1925
James Kemper, Sr. named president of Commerce Trust Company. W.T. Kemper buys Kansas City, Mexico & Orient Railroad.

1928
Commerce Trust opens first 24-hour check clearing operation in the country. **W.T. Kemper** sells Kansas City, Mexico & Orient Railroad to the Santa Fe Railroad.

1920

1930

1921
W.T. Kemper becomes chairman of newly consolidated Commerce Trust; Women's Department is established and overseen by **Mrs. Ralph Beebe.**

1922
W.T. Kemper sells his interest in Commerce to **Theodore Gary** for more than $200 per share. **James Kemper, Sr.** begins working at Commerce.

1932
W.T. Kemper reacquires Commerce Bank for $86 per share.

1933
Commerce Bank survives run during Great Depression. **W.T. Kemper** hands out apples to cheer up people waiting in line to withdraw their deposits. Banking Act of 1933 creates the FDIC system.

OUTLINE OF THE HISTORY
of
Commerce Trust Company
KANSAS CITY

FEDERAL DEPOSIT 1933 INSURANCE CORPORATION

FINANCE

Truman May Group All U.S. Loan Agencies

1944
James Kemper, Sr. joins with other community leaders to found Midwest Research Institute, helping Kansas City develop new industries.

1946
James Kemper, Jr. begins work at the First National Bank of Independence, controlled by the Kemper family. Later that year, he moves to Commerce Trust Company.

OUR 85TH YEAR
1865 1950
COMMERCE TRUST CO.

1953
Commerce installs landmark clock at corner of 10th and Walnut. With a weight of approximately two tons, many terrified pedestrians refuse to walk under it.

COMMERCE TRUST CO.
MEMBER FEDERAL DEPOSIT INSURANCE CORPORATION
Banking is our Business, and **TRUST** is our middle name

1940

1950

1955
Commerce leads financing for TWA overhaul base. (By 1972, TWA is Kansas City's largest employer.) **James Kemper, Jr.** becomes president of the bank. **James Kemper, Sr. and Arthur Eisenhower** dedicate first "electric stairs" in Kansas City, installed in Commerce Trust Building.

1958
Capital for Business is formed to make investments in small to midsize manufacturing and distribution companies.

TWA

LIFETIME PASS
GOOD FOR UNLIMITED USAGE ON THE
Commerce Trust Company
GLIDING ELECTRIC STAIRS

This pass is our good guarantee
That you can ESCALATE for free.
May your ups-and-downs be smooth and near,
And restful on your legs and feet!

150 YEARS OF BUILDING COMMERCE

Commerce Trust Company

1965
Commerce Tower opens at 911 Main in Kansas City. Top of the Tower Restaurant occupies the 30th floor.

Commerce purchases Midwestern license for BankAmericard— predecessor of VISA bank card.

1966
Commerce organizes bank holding company, Commerce Bancshares. The next year, it starts acquiring banks in Missouri.

1971
Commerce Trust Company changes name to Commerce Bank, NA. Commerce Bancshares begins publicly trading on NASDAQ.

Assets pass $1 billion.

1979
Installation of the first Commerce Bank ATM, located in Springfield, Missouri.

1978
Commerce acquires first affiliate bank in St. Louis— Manchester Financial.

David Kemper joins Commerce in Commercial Lending.

1960

1970

Above, **President Harry S. Truman** *autographs steel girders at the topping out ceremony for the new Commerce Tower. Right,* **James Kemper, Jr.** *at the Commerce Tower dedication ceremony.*

Now: A wonderful new world of banking

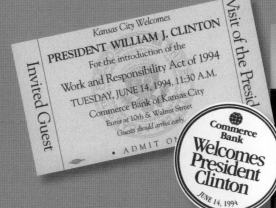

Commerce Bancshares, Inc.

1990
Commerce sells its interest in Commerce Tower.

1982
David Kemper becomes president and chief operating officer. **Jonathan Kemper** joins bank.

1984
Commerce Bank of Omaha is established for credit card business. Later that year, Commerce introduces "Special Connections"—first card having both credit and ATM functions.

1991
President George H. W. Bush gives Commerce "E Star" Award for exports.

1994
President Bill Clinton announces welfare reform in a speech given in the Walnut lobby, at the Commerce Trust Company building in Kansas City.

1980

1990

1983
Commerce acquires County Tower Corp. in St. Louis.

1985
Commerce acquires First National Bank of St. Joseph from the FDIC.

1986
Construction completed on the Commerce Bank building at 1000 Walnut Street in Kansas City.

1992
Commerce acquires First Peoria Corporation, which was originally founded in 1863.

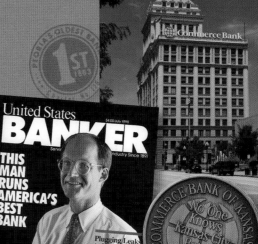

150 YEARS OF BUILDING COMMERCE

AMERICA'S BEST BANK. AGAIN.
Commerce Bank

2003
David Kemper rings bell at NASDAQ. Commerce Bancshares was among the first companies listed on NASDAQ.

2011
David Kemper testifies before House subcommittee on effects of Interchange legislation.

2013
John Woods Kemper named president and chief operating officer.

Commerce acquires Summit Bank in Tulsa and Oklahoma City.

+ LONG TERM VIEW + ONE TEAM + INTEGRITY + CUSTOMER FOCUSED + EXCELLENCE +
Commerce Bank

Commerce Bank

| 2000 | | | | 2010 | |

2001
The Commerce Trust Building added to the National Register of Historic Places; renovation completed.

2007
Commerce acquires banks in Tulsa, Oklahoma, and Aurora, Colorado.

2009
Following the 2008 banking crisis, Commerce chooses not to receive TARP Funds from the federal government.

2014
Next-generation high-tech banking center opens in St. Louis featuring innovative approach to customer service.

Transaction Center

CALL
SEND

FDIC

Here today.
Here tomorrow.

commercebank.com/soundness Commerce Bank

BUILDING COMMERCE
STRENGTH · COMMUNITY · INNOVATION
150 YEARS

2015
Commerce Bank commemorates 150th anniversary: has $24 billion in assets; operates in eight key markets, with more than 190 branches, plus three additional commercial offices in central U.S.; employs more than 4,800 people.

COMMERCE BANCSHARES: GROWTH THROUGH THE YEARS

Commerce Bancshares was incorporated in 1966 as a registered bank holding company to acquire and operate banks within Missouri and, after 1992, throughout the surrounding region. Since that time, the Commerce family of banks has joined and grown with the 63 banks and communities listed below.

1967
Citizens Bank *Springfield, MO*

1968
Chariton County Exchange Bank *Brunswick, MO*
Citizens Bank *Joplin, MO*

1969
Citizens National Bank *Kirksville, MO*
Columbia National Bank *Columbia, MO*
The Mechanics Bank *St. Joseph, MO*
The Union State Bank
- *Kirkwood, MO*
- *St. Charles, MO*
- *University City, MO*

1970
American Trust Company *Hannibal, MO*
First State Bank *Bonne Terre, MO*
Mechanics Bank & Trust *Moberly, MO*
Mexico Savings Bank *Mexico, MO*
State Bank *Lebanon, MO*
Tipton Farmers Bank *Tipton, MO*

1971
State Bank *Poplar Bluff, MO*
Willard Bank *Willard, MO*

1972
Blue Hills Bank of Commerce *Kansas City, MO*
Clay County State Bank *Excelsior Springs, MO*
Fenton Bank *Fenton, MO*

1973
Citizens Bank *Festus, MO*
Citizens National Bank *Harrisonville, MO*
Lexington Bank and Trust *Lexington, MO*

1974
Exchange Bank *Kahoka, MO*
Farmers and Merchants Bank *Bolivar, MO*
Valley Bank *Florissant, MO*

1975
Barry County Bank *Cassville, MO*

1978
Manchester Bank *St. Louis, MO*

1980
American Security Bank *Pacific, MO*
Spanish Lake Bank & Trust *Spanish Lake, MO*

1982
Plaza Bank & Trust *Kansas City, MO*
Wentzville State Bank *Wentzville, MO*

1984
County Tower Bank
- *Arnold, MO*
- *Chesterfield, MO*
- *Clayton, MO*
- *House Springs, MO*
- *Louisiana, MO*
- *Manchester, MO*
- *Richmond Heights, MO*
- *Tower Grove, MO*
- *Webster Groves, MO*

1985
First National Bank* *St. Joseph, MO*

1990
Blue Valley Savings*
- *Independence, MO*
- *St. Joseph, MO*

1992
AMCORE Bank, *Pekin, IL*
First Exchange Bank*
- *Cape Girardeau, MO*
- *Fredericktown, MO*
- *Mound City, MO*
First National Bank *Bonner Springs, KS*
First National Bank
- *Bloomington-Normal, IL*
- *Pekin, IL*
- *Peoria, IL*
Lenexa National Bank *Lenexa, KS*
Security State Bank *Republic, MO*

1993
Farmers State Bank and Trust *Hays, KS*
Lawrence County Bank *Aurora, MO*
Manufacturers State Bank *Leavenworth, KS*
Union National Bank *Manhattan, KS*

1994
Commercial Bank *Liberty, MO*
Bank of Kansas *Lawrence, KS*
Moniteau National Bank *California, MO*
Twin City State Bank *Kansas City, KS*
Walnut Valley State Bank *El Dorado, KS*

1995
Chillicothe State Bank *Chillicothe, IL*
Cotton Exchange Bank *Kennett, MO*
The Peoples Bank *Bloomington, IL*
Union National Bank *Wichita, KS*

1997
Citizens National Bank *Independence, KS*
Shawnee State Bank *Mission, KS*

1998
City National Bank *Pittsburg, KS*
Columbus State Bank *Columbus, KS*
Fidelity of Garden City
- *Fidelity State Bank* *Garden City, KS*
- *Heritage Bank* *Olathe, KS*

2001
Centennial Bank *St. Ann, MO*

2006
Boone National Savings & Loan *Columbia, MO*
West Pointe Bank and Trust *Belleville, IL*

2007
Bank South *Tulsa, OK*
Commerce Bank *Aurora, CO*

2013
Summit Bank
- *Oklahoma City, OK*
- *Tulsa, OK*

*Acquired through FDIC or RTC

WOODS AND KEMPER FAMILY TREE

T hrough six generations, the Woods and Kemper families have been leaders in Commerce Bank.

This family tree illustrates the relationships between those family members who have held leadership roles in the bank; please note it is not a complete list of all Woods and Kemper family members.

☐ Current or former Commerce Executive.

Dr. William Stone Woods
1840-1917

Albina McBride

Rufus H. Crosby
1834-1891

Nettie Kendall

Arthur Grissom

Julia McBride Woods

W.T. Kemper
1865-1938

Charlotte Crosby

Gladys Woods Grissom

James Madison Kemper, Sr.
1894-1965

R. Crosby Kemper, Sr.
1892-1972

W.T. Kemper, Jr.
1902-1989

James Madison Kemper, Jr.
1921-

Mildred Lane

Laura Kemper Fields
1948-2014

Jonathan McBride Kemper
1953-

David Woods Kemper
1950-

Dorothy Jannarone

John Woods Kemper
1978-

ACKNOWLEDGMENTS

I wish to thank members of the Kemper family—notably Jonathan, David, John and James Jr.—for being generous with their time, recollections and thoughts about the history of their family and their business. Kirby Upjohn, executive director of the David Woods Kemper Foundation, was especially helpful on this front, as well. In addition, Terri Hurd, Molly Hyland and Robin Trafton of Commerce Bank's communications staff were tireless in helping me research the book and in arranging interviews, providing context, getting me oriented and keeping me on course.

I am especially appreciative of the many Commerce executives and current and former employees, board members and customers who took the time to tell me their stories: Kevin Barth, Henry and Tom Bloch, Steve Broun, John Brown, Jeff Burik, John Capps, Bayard Clark, Wade Edmundson, Mark Fishel, Sara Foster, Harvey Fried, Loura Gilbert, David Glass, John Himmel, Irving O. Hockaday, Jr., Carl Hudgins, Patty Kellerhals, Charles Kim, Diana Knight, Charles Kopke, Jim Lewien, David Lindsey, James Linn, Don Mason, Bob Matthews, Johnny Morris, James Nutter, Sr., Mike Petrie, Ken Ragan, Bob Rauscher, Jay Reardon, Michael Robie, John Stieven, Morton Sosland, Ray Stranghoener, Bill Sullins, Andy Taylor, Warren Weaver, Robert West and Mark Wrighton.

Derek Donovan of the *Kansas City Star* should be recognized for his ability to find old newspaper clippings about Commerce and the Kemper family. The staff of the Kansas City Public Library was particularly helpful in tracking down old publications not available elsewhere; the library's senior special collections librarian, Jeremy Drouin, cheerfully found and provided access to historical photographs. The same can be said of Steve Noll, executive director of the Jackson County Historical Society, who patiently let the publisher rummage through the archive in Independence and supplied many high-resolution images from the society's collection.

Special appreciation to Christopher Gordon at the Missouri Historical Society, Bruce Bettinger at Dolphin Archival Printing and the kind people at the American Bankers Association, the Federal Deposit Insurance Corporation, the Federal Reserve Bank of Kansas City, the Mildred Lane Kemper Art Museum, the TWA Museum and the Kansas City Royals for providing information, documents and photographs. Finally, thanks to Glen Hansen for the use of his beautiful paintings on the book's cover and to Scott Hepler for his gorgeous photography.   — Chris Roush, July 2015

ABOUT THE AUTHOR

Chris Roush is senior associate dean for undergraduate studies and the Walter E. Hussman, Sr. professor in business journalism at the School of Media and Journalism at the University of North Carolina-Chapel Hill. He has won awards for his teaching at the campus, state and national level, and he is considered to be among the world's leading authorities on business journalism. He has written nine books, including the corporate histories of The Home Depot, Alex Lee Inc., Pacific Coast Feather Co. and Progress Energy.

PHOTO CREDITS:

All images courtesy of Commerce Bancshares, with the following exceptions:

Cover, oil painting by Glen Hansen
Full-title page, 28 (Long-Bell), 44 © Wilborn & Associates
Pages 11, 12, 17, 91, 92 © Mark McDonald
Pages 13, 73 The *Kansas City Star*
Page 16, © Ian Adams
Page 18, George Caleb Bingham, *Daniel Boone Escorting Settlers through the Cumberland Gap*, 1851-52. Oil on canvas, 36 1/2" x 50 1/4". Mildred Lane Kemper Art Museum, Washington University, St. Louis. Gift of Nathaniel Phillips, 1890.
Page 20 (map), from the collection of Jonathan Kemper
Pages 22, 27, 47 (map), Missouri Valley Special Collections, Kansas City Public Library, Kansas City, Missouri
Pages 24, 32 (speech), 33*, 38 (newspaper), 57 (Kemper family), The Jackson County Historical Society Archives Collection
Page 28 (logging camp), International Paper Company Knowledge Resource Center Library and Historical Archives
Page 35* (both), Courtesy Harry S. Truman Presidential Library
Page 42, Bank Archives, Federal Reserve Bank of Kansas City
Page 62 (Greenlease), AP – New York
Page 64, © Kevin Sink Photography
Page 66 (Kauffman), Courtesy of the Ewing Marion Kauffman Foundation
Page 66 (check), Courtesy of the Kansas City Royals
Page 67* (both), The TWA Museum
Page 84, © Walter Bibikow/JAI/Corbis
Page 89, Dorn Communications, Inc.
Page 90, Washington University in St. Louis
Page 93, Provided by Enterprise Rent-a-Car
Page 97, Clinton Presidential Library
Page 100, Courtesy of OSF HealthCare
Page 118, Courtesy of Missouri Department of Natural Resources / Tower Grove East Historic District National Register Nomination
Page 128, © Michael Mihalevich, photographer

Photo also appears in timeline

INDEX